Edinburgh Review

104 Paolozzi: Life and Work

Edinburgh Review

22a Buccleuch Place, Edinburgh, EH8 9LN
tel / fax: 0131 651 1415
Edinburgh.Review@ed.ac.uk

MANAGING EDITOR — Alex Thomson
DISTRIBUTION MANAGER — Catherine McDonald
REVIEWS EDITOR — Matthew Reason
STUDENT BOARD — Ross Alloway, Stephen Carruthers, Alice Ferrebe,
    Julie Hilder, Katy Mahood, Catherine McDonald, Matthew
    Reason
EDITORIAL BOARD — Cairns Craig, Kimberly Hutchings, A.L.
    Kennedy, Andrew O'Hagan, Christopher Whyte
COVER DESIGN — Siân Braes
FRONT COVER IMAGE — 'Mr Peanut' (detail), screenprint, by Eduardo
    Paolozzi, reproduced by permission of Scottish National Gallery
    of Modern Art
LOGO — Alasdair Gray

ISSN 0267 6672
ISBN 1 85933 201 3

PRINTED AND BOUND in the UK by Antony Rowe Ltd.,
    Bumper's Farm, Chippenham, Wiltshire
PUBLISHED by the Centre for the History of Ideas in Scotland,
    University of Edinburgh
SUPPORTED by

THE SCOTTISH ARTS COUNCIL

National or municipal art?

STRANGE TIMES IN the art world. So far this year we've seen not only the opening of the Tate Modern at Bankside, as well as several other major gallery projects reaching completion in London; but also the increased running-down of Britain's local museums and galleries, as they fail to compete with the brighter, flasher, sexier or just, well, bigger projects. Meanwhile the National Galleries of Scotland have put on display their latest toy, ten million pounds worth of Botticelli. 'Who would have guessed that the National Gallery of Scotland would ever possess a genuine Botticelli?' asked Timothy Clifford. Who indeed.

Six years ago, Murdo Macdonald's editorial in issue 91 of *Edinburgh Review*, was a blistering attack on the proposal to site a National Gallery of Scottish Art in Glasgow. While that particular ill-fated project never came about, the publication of his excellent little book *Scottish Art* gives us an opportunity to reflect on what, if anything, has changed for the management of art in Scotland, if that's not itself a tautology.*

His new book is a brief but expansive survey of art in Scotland, largely focused on the last three hundred years, but with brief nods to prehistoric and early Christian work: as you might expect with Thames & Hudson, the book is lavishly illustrated. The underlying tension of the book, as to whether this is the art of Scotland, those works produced within a specific geographical area which, or whether there is anything specifically 'Scottish' about the works, is never really resolved: read sympathetically this seems to me a fruitful solution to a difficult problem.

Certainly, had Macdonald actually set out to answer the question on the book's back cover, 'What makes Scottish art Scottish?', the book would have

* *Scottish Art* — **Murdo Macdonald, Thames & Hudson, pbk £7.95, ISBN 0 500 20333 4**

lost much of its impact and authority. Instead he demonstrates that Scottish culture, like any culture, makes no sense considered in isolation, but is in a continuous process of translation and influence with others: he draws particular attention to the interaction between Scotland and France in the visual arts. In the same issue of *Edinburgh Review* that I have already referred to, Macdonald argues for the study of visual art in Scotland 'to sustain understanding of the *interconnected diversity* which *contributes* to the identity of people in Scotland' (my emphasis) and this could equally serve as an epigraph for his new book.

It is certainly difficult to argue with Macdonald's extended 'Epilogue,' subtitled 'Deconstructing Stereotypes and Reappropriating Symbols,' in which he briefly addresses the diverse aims and approaches of contemporary Scottish artists. There's enough potential material in this one short section of the book for a much larger work of some significance. The subtitle suggests that the question of nationality must remain open for these artists. Which poses the problem of how we are to relate the vivid and divergent renewal of contemporary art in Scotland with the relentlessly national rhetoric of cultural management. Not only does Timothy Clifford talk of investing in art 'for the nation,' but the largest exhibition of contemporary art in Scotland for some time, spread across a number of Edinburgh galleries earlier this year was called 'The British Art Show 5.'

I am tempted to suggest the pragamtic solution that artists should be free to change their nationality to whatever the person paying for or exhibiting their work wants it to be. But there's a deeper issue here? Should we still be thinking about national art at all, or is this now as meaningless a concept as the Botticelli purchase suggests. Even if it makes the National Galleries the envy of other curators the world over, can this painting really be said to be vital to the cultural health of the nation? Whatever contribution a painting which has only been in Scotland since 1859, and which hasn't been publicly displayed for more than a decade, may make to the future of the nation, it certainly can't be said to have been vital *yet.*

The positive news represented by Macdonald's book is that it is now no longer possible to presume that Scotland does not have any tradition in the visual arts. Perhaps now we can turn back to the pools and eddies in the stream of tradition, to deepen our understanding of its microhistories, but also of the points of resistance and fracture in that tradition, the faultlines which open it up to the outside. Beside the points of connection and translation there must also be points of disturbance, in which the narrative of national art can be challenged.

I'd like to suggest that Paolozzi's work might be such a point. But isn't there a contradiction here? As Duncan Macmillan asks in his essay, 'why should one artist stand out so clearly from all the rest [...]? A Royal Academician, the Queen's Sculptor in Scotland, [is] this not just ducking choice, taking the safe option with an establishment figure?' So isn't Paolozzi too ubiquitous, too well-known, too, say it quietly, *respected*?

Take a look at the texts collected here by and about Paolozzi, and several points are obvious. Firstly that while always working with tradition, and paying explicit attention to local traditions, in preparing his public sculptures, Paolozzi's work can not be ascribed to a national position. How could it be, for the boy who grew up speaking four languages on Albert Street in Edinburgh, has lived and worked in France, Germany, the United States and even, *quelle horreur*, England.

Secondly, the strength and consistency of Paolozzi's work seems to lie at least in part in its concern for a public context, and for a frustration of any attempt to interpret it as a private project. A quick glance at the collection of texts collected here concerning the 'Manuscript for Monte Cassino' sculpture at the top of Leith Walk in Edinburgh will show that there is no easy jump to be made from life to work for Paolozzi.

Not only that, but the range of issues which such a sculpture engages can not easily be reduced either to a matter of artistic forms, or of themes. It must be read in terms of both local and international contexts, as well as the traditions of Western thought and representation (and of Western thought *as* representation) which are still dominant today, and Paolozzi's consistent concern for technology, waste and violence. The personality (or nationality, even) of the artist becomes radically contingent to the work itself, even if they must still be inscribed there.

The public sphere itself is created and maintained by work of this nature, which presumes a mass public audience who can respond to the work without further instruction (and which seeks to play a part in social space, rather than the institutional space of the gallery). It is a sphere of debate, of polemic and critique, not just of the institution of legislation.

I want to suggest one further distinction, to clarify the issue here. Could we see Paolozzi's work as *municipal* art, rather than in terms of nation? The difference I have in mind would be between the opening of the public sphere and its closure, by submission to the master narratives of nation or of community. For the discourse of 'nation' and 'community' conforms to a romantic paradigm in which individual interiority is elevated above all else; these values being neatly reflected in the inward-looking state which wraps itself in the rhetoric of national community.

The challenge of Paolozzi's work as municipal art would be to insist on the dialogue within the public sphere that determines a more enlightened understanding of the social. What distinguishes Adam Smith's *Theory of Moral Sentiments*, after all, is its relentless focus on the position of the spectator: not dwelling on the subjectivity, the 'identity,' of the participants, but on the circulation of the moral gaze itself. Or we might think of Alasdair Gray's demonstration of the importance of municipal action in *Poor Things*, a book whose real hero is the city of Glasgow itself. As Victoria McCandless's 1914 letter to posterity comments: 'Glasgow is an exciting place for a dedicated Socialist. Even in its earlier Liberal phase it set the world an example through the municipal development of public resources.'

The municipal stands not only for the preservation of historical records as a local or regional project, and thus for the constitution of resistance to the rhetoric of national unity, and a stand against the public-funded accumulation of speculative capital, whether by Botticelli, or Saatchi-era Britart. But it also represents the pragmatic and easily forgotten projects such as drains and clean water — and in particular for the potential of education — which will have changed the lives of more people than any work of art will ever have.

What has become of Victoria McCandless's optimism? That debate must continue: and many of the pieces collected in this issue make their own contribution. Turn to many of the essays here on Paolozzi, which accompany a selection of his own writings; or the reviews of Neil Davidson or Slavoj Zizek's renewals of the Socialist tradition: listen to the many voices of the poetry and prose collected here; and to Ronald Turnbull's plea for a revival of debate in devolved Scotland.

This issue would not have been possible without the help, not only of all the contributors, and especially of Robin Spencer, Fiona Pearson and Halla Beloff, but also of Helen Nicoll at the Scottish National Gallery of Modern Art. Our next issue is themed around theatre in Scotland; anyone interested in contributing should contact us by the middle of September.

Texts for Monte Casino

Eduardo Paolozzi

INTRODUCTORY NOTE: Eduardo Paolozzi's sculpture, 'The Manuscript of Monte Cassino' stands at the top of Leith Walk, not far from where he grew up. These texts and photographs provide a revealing set of contexts for the piece; not only autobiographical, but also artistic and political. The pieces have been deliberately left as fragments and each is preceded by a note indicating its source. Some, but not all, of the texts will appear in the forthcoming collection of Paolozzi's writings from Oxford University Press.

MEMOIRS

These extracts come from memoirs, dictated in 1994, and recorded by a publisher with a view to publishing the artist's autobiography.

MY FATHER decided that I should go to the local school, Leith Walk School, as soon as I was old enough to be accepted, perhaps age 4½. This was in order that I could come home for lunch and run back again joining my companions who had been confined to the playground with their sandwiches in all weathers.

Gallons of milk were delivered from an outside farm arriving on a lorry in heavy milk churns and poured directly into a large vessel, copper bottomed on a specially welded stand, the farmer bringing at the same time a live rooster, which lived in the back lavatory until being slaughtered on Saturday night, to be simmered all night in tomatoes for lunch after mass at Sunday midday, cooked in the traditional way of the village Viticuso. This enormous dish would emerge in different forms over the next four days, the sauce being used for tagliatelli or risotto.

This all took place in a room which was used to the point that the room was worn out — everything was cracked and broken and patched whereas the apartment above the shop was underused. The cast-iron range was always pristine and hardly ever used, the fire only lit when there was illness.

A thousand activities took place in the back shop, including piano practice, my mother cooking endlessly the same dishes that her mother made; and even though a certain form of affluence began to appear, certain village tasks were exercised, like making sheets from bleached flour-bags or rendering down fat from pieces of pork bought at the Saturday night market.

My grandfather's shop was of a different kind and situated on Leith Walk itself, like their apartment, only a block away from where I was born. On select days I would take my grandfather's lunch of cold pasta between two soup plates wrapped in a tea-towel. Should I have dropped this precious load the consequences would have been too severe to contemplate.

Getting to school in the morning was always a problem. Unlike my contemporaries, I would have to stay up until my parents were ready to close the shop, which really meant that the street had gone to bed. The tenement houses opposite were all gas-lit and in most cases the curtains were never drawn so it was not uncommon to see life going on through the windows. My own bedroom still had an active gas-jet which I would light occasionally, a split second of dangerous fun. Several framed pictures of the Madonna on the walls, images more or less positioned, were there more for formal reasons than as icons of deep belief.

My father, as did his ancestors in Viticuso, left most of the praying to the women, and made only an occasional guest appearance at some Italian national service at St Mary's Cathedral dressed always in a black suit, waistcoat, and boots with a stiff collar and knitted tie. Being a soldier had a marked effect on my father, and going out with him to an occasion at the Italian Club was preceded by an hour's preparation for the family, like making an appearance on the parade-ground. It was important always to

Portrait of Eduardo Paolozzi with his sister
by permission of Scottish National Gallery of Modern Art

hurry back from school and be given the task for the day, ending sometimes between ten and midnight according to the seasons.

Much later on in life, when my three daughters were growing up in the country, they experienced a life unlike my own childhood, or that of my wife, including the reading of tales after their bath shepherded by the Danish au-pair girl anxious not to be delayed for her rendezvous with a friend in Clacton-on-Sea. The door of my bedroom was never closed and I could see a large clock on the kitchen wall which my father wound up himself. This was a nightly duty and the first thing I saw when I woke, telling me, this eloquent mechanical friend, that I had six or seven minutes left to get dressed and get to school on time. Not difficult if the jersey and clothes had been prepared the night before with a shirt and tie in its jersey allowing, like a fireman in a contest, for the fast execution of his duties, a transformation from a sleeping figure to a running image going down Albert Street and up Leith Walk in a matter of minutes.

The wardrobe had been made by my father who was endlessly, creatively restless, and on the inner panels of the doors as a contrast to the icons on the wall I pasted images from the world that fascinated me: cigarette-cards of locomotives and aeroplanes, and double spreads of images from magazines of cross sections, or even a section view of the London underground.

Coming back from school, I would find both my parents deeply involved in tasks, my mother crushing by hand a barrel of grapes bought cheaply, the grapes being packed in some cork granules. If it was high summer, my father would be in the cellar making gallons of custard.

In wintertime, when ice-cream sales were slower my father would make a radio from a blueprint in a magazine. This was a continuation of some enthusiasm enjoyed during his period of military service. Contrary to some views, doing obligatory military service was often a period of enlightenment for the underprivileged boys from the mountain villages. By the time I was 15, there was a radio in every room of our flat, and it is true that through the radio a curious sense of London developed.

By the age of 10 I could speak four languages and it never appeared to be a trial. I could shuffle from one to the other without any sense of embarrassment or difficulty. My parents spoke their village dialect to me, and on going to school I learned to speak proper English. And yet the language in the streets was somewhat different and in its broadest sense not unlike the same accents of Glasgow.

The Italian community in Edinburgh at that time was bound together by an Italian Club staffed by a teacher and an official sent specially from Italy. Two days a week I would go to the Italian Club for proper Italian conducted by a goddess sent from Italy. This formidable creature always wore shiny stockings and wonderful shoes unlike her duller cousins, the teachers at Leith Walk School. On two days a week Italian lessons were given after normal school times.

[...]

On the 10th of June Italy declared war. I was still at school at the time (Holy Cross Academy) and came back in the early afternoon to find my father in the back shop listening to a radio of his own construction, listening to Radio Firenze which at that time had a call signal of a nightingale. That afternoon Mussolini made his famous speech declaring war on the Allies.

My mother and I could tell by my father's reaction that a series of solemn duties had to be performed. Hung on the walls were all my certificates from my summertimes at the camps on the Adriatic including a large map of Abyssinia where my father used to put the flags of the advancing Italian armies from the North and from the South — General Badoglio from the North and General Graziani from the South. Every day the Italian radio announced the progress of the various regimental groups. My father assumed that by destroying all Fascist memorabilia — certificates and photographs of our Italian connections — that the local police would leave us unharmed.

From an early age I was expected, according to our tradition, to work. After school I would put on a khaki coat and attend to the various tasks involved in running a small ice-cream shop with ancillary sales of sweets and cigarettes. Like running a small ship, the tasks were endless — cleaning, washing, and scrubbing the cellar floor where the milk was boiled and the custard was made for the ice cream. If not working in the front shop, certainly from an early age I helped my mother. If only by osmosis, by the age of sixteen I had become an expert cook of Italian regional cooking and very proficient — as good as my father — at making ice cream.

The back shop by this time was worn out due to a small family having lived there doing everything for long periods of time. My mother spent most of her life there and like any peasant woman from her village, cooked and prepared food in the style inherited from her mother; who in turn carried out her duties as if still living in the mountains of central Italy.

The back shop was a violent contrast with the flat two flights above the shop, which was under-used and consequently the linoleum and all the fittings were pristine and always appeared to be new. It seemed advisable on this momentous day to move up there as the evening started to darken.

Consequently, under the cover of darkness roving mobs started all over Edinburgh to smash and loot those Italian premises that for decades had been a crucial part of the Scottish street and social life.

The carefully arranged shop windows usually had been 'dressed' by a visiting confectionery representative — with sundae dishes holding ice creams fixed in perpetuity in some composition material and chocolates made of composition materials in glass bowls filled with crêpe paper. In the shop itself, on glass shelves backed by mirrors, were glass jars containing the real thing. In very little time this world, which had existed for a decade and a half, was reduced to splintered wood and small pieces of broken glass.

During those incredible moments we listened, my father, mother, sister, and I, to those unexpected noises of hatred and violence. And shortly afterwards, perhaps mercifully, two detectives and a policeman came to take my father away. They seemed to be quite respectful and apologetic and an hour later, with equal kindness, I was escorted to Saughton Prison.

It had already been decided that the Edinburgh Italians would be put in the remand wing, it being empty at the time. This meant that everyone had their own cell. The wooden floor of the cell had been freshly beeswaxed and looked reasonable with its pink china mug and pottery chamber-pot. Next morning all the cell doors were opened for breakfast and we could see our fellows. A few were familiar faces and others were complete strangers who had been trawled in from the outlying parts of Edinburgh. There were a few still in their Army uniforms, and, curiously, three in the uniform of a highland regiment.

My first visitor was my Uncle Carl, my mother's half-brother, who for some bizarre reason hadn't been picked up, with news of my mother and sister who had been ordered to live some thirty miles from the coast in case my mother sent messages to enemy submarines. This was a strange time in British history. Being given the status of remand prisoners, we were allowed to wear our own clothes, have food sent in from outside, and perhaps more importantly, newspapers, which at that time described in detail the progress of the Battle of Britain.

The notion that Britain was struggling for its life made any sense of rancour amongst us seem unnecessary and uncalled for. It has been well chronicled, this period in time, and as the preoccupation with the threat of invasion evaporated, so the political tension eased and the prisoners in Saughton Jail were slowly let out to attempt to pursue their previous

occupations: in my own case to visit my mother and sister at Innerleithen on the Borders.

Innerleithen at the time was a training station for an elite Polish group who later no doubt perished on the slopes of Monte Cassino. Ironically, my father had said when war was declared that this small Italian village would be well out of the way of the strife and destruction, being in the middle of the Gothic Line. In fact, the departing German Army placed land-mines in every house destroying the entire village on their departure.

THEFTS FROM ITALIAN SHOPS IN EDINBURGH

From the Edinburgh *Evening News*, Thursday June 13th 1940

'It was a foolish thing to do, but someone shouted, "The window is open; come on, boys, sweets for nothing," and I just went in,' said John Brownlee, 7 Lyne Street, when he admitted, along with Andrew Bathgate, 17 Rossie Place, he stole a 5lb jar of sweets and a quantity of loose sweets from a shop occupied by Alphonso Crolla at 128 Easter Road, early on Tuesday morning. They were each fined £1, with the alternative of ten days imprisonment, at Edinburgh Burgh Court today by Councillor Gilzean.

George M'Gregor, 5 Albert Street, was also fined £1, with the alternative of ten days' imprisonment, when he pleaded guilty to stealing four bottles of aerated waters and a glass jar containing sweets from a shop owned by Rudolph Paolozzi.

For stealing a carton of chocolate spread from a shop at 24 Tolbooth Wynd occupied by Michale Inerelli on Monday night, Councillor Gilzean imposed a fine of £1, with the option of ten days imprisonment, on Murdoch Robertson, 7-8 James Place, Leith, who admitted the offence.

PROPOSAL FOR SCULPTURE AT PICARDY PLACE, LEITH WALK

Following improvement plans which had been drawn up for Leith Walk, Edinburgh, in 1986, including a new layout for pedestrians and traffic, the artist was commissioned by the City of Edinburgh to develop proposals for public sculpture outside St Mary's Cathedral. The initial proposal dates from 1988 and includes architectural and carved elements, but these were subsequently eliminated. The sculpture was installed in July 1991.

THE HISTORY of the Leith Walk area is firmly united with my own autobiography. I worshipped at St. Mary's Cathedral, shopped in the stores formerly at the top of the Walk, dreamed in the local cinema, and played around the Calton Hill columns and the Leith Goods Depot (Leith Central Station). These areas are sources of inspiration for the sculpture I propose for Picardy Place.

Cast bronze column fragments echo the monument on Calton Hill as well as the grandeur of the cathedral; arrangements of pavingstones call to mind the vanished shops and cinema; stones from Leith Central Station, currently being demolished, bring the actuality of the station to Leith Walk; geometric shapes provide a background for other elements while referring to local buildings.

The aim of the sculpture is to create a 'social sculpture' — a calm haven of rest within a busy commercial area, a bit of quiet beside an endless stream of pedestrian and vehicular traffic. The sculpture together with trees and landscaping should provide a place to stop or meet on the way to shops, a peninsula from which to view Calton Hill or the rest of the Leith Walk community.

These references come through a series of metaphors on a human scale — a union of Edinburgh architecture with the natural geology of surrounding hills-a suggestion of abstract geometry and recognizable elements, of ancient memories and shared childhood experiences.

MATERIALS
bronze
preferably locally cast
cast iron could be a less expensive — although a less sympathetic material bronze takes on the history of its environment, becoming brightly polished when stroked or sat upon, taking on a green tinge where ignored
stones
retrieved from Leith Central Station — natural or carved
local granite, pavingstones
trees and other plantings

COSTS
At this stage the concept of the sculpture is firm in my mind. Individual elements can, however, be altered to accommodate the budget. There is little point, however, in creating a work too small to be noticed. With my ideal number of bronze and carved elements included the budget for the work from final acceptance of the proposal to complete installation would be £98,000. By reducing the number of cast elements and economizing with 'found' elements it could, however, be possible to create a work for approximately £44,000.

SOURCES
The journal of Johann Gottfried Herder
Athanasius Kircher, *A Renaissance Man & the Quest for Lost Knowledge*
Robert Fludd, *Hermetic Philosopher, Surveyor Two Worlds*
Kalender Bauten, *Astronomical Monuments from India, Mexico and Peru*

[Note: When the Edinburgh sculpture was conceived Paolozzi was also working on the exhibition *Arche Noah* for Munich, at which time he became increasingly interested in medieval and Renaissance mysticism, and language theory about early man.]

MASSIVE SCULPTURES INSTALLED AT PICARDY PLACE

The Manuscript of Monte Cassino, **which consists of three massive bronze sculptures of an ankle, a foot, and a hand, was cast by the Raimund Kittl Foundry, Dusseldorf, and installed in July 1991. From the press release, issued by the City of Edinburgh District Council, dated 9 July 1991.**

I WAS BORN in Crown Place at the foot of Leith Walk next to the now demolished Leith Central Station. My grandfather had his ice-cream shop quite nearby on Leith Walk. Further up, my father's shop was established at Albert Street near Pilrig. From the age of four until twelve, I went to Leith Walk School. From age twelve until 1940, I was a pupil at Holy Cross Academy. As a child, I went to the Catholic church in Leith or to Sunday mass at St Mary's Metropolitan Cathedral.

Edinburgh, with its fine historic architecture must be complemented with works of suitable grandeur, with sculpture of the right scale and material on a theme that reflects the everlasting inspiration that the City has drawn upon from classical models. This was the case when I was a student at the Edinburgh College of Art.

On the site I can see these very parts of the landscape that were the backcloth of my childhood. A great deal has disappeared, which makes it a privilege to add something significant to what might have become an urban gap.

The title of the three sculptures is *The Manuscript of Monte Cassino*. This is inscribed on the hand with a date and signature:

MS. OF MONTE CASSINO
Ad Paulum diaconum

Hinc celer egrediens facili, mea carta, volatu
per silvas, colles, valles quoque prepete cursu
alma deo cari Benedicti tecta require.
Est nam certa quies fessis venientibus illuc,
hic olus hospitibus, piscis hic, panis abundans;
pax pia, mens humilis, pulcra et concordia fratrum,
laus, amor et cultus Christi simul omnibus horis.

MS. OF MONTE CASSINO
Written to Paul the Deacon at Monte Cassino

Across the hills and in the valley's shade,
Alone the small script goes,
Seeking for Bendict's beloved roof,
Where waits its sure repose.
They come and find, the tired travellers,
Green herbs and ampple bread,
Quiet and brothers' love and humbleness,
Christ's peace on every head.

(trans. Helen Waddell, *Medieval Latin Lyrics*)

The entire text in Latin is inscribed round the ankle and foot. This serves a double link between the Cathedral and the origins of not only my father and grandfather but to many Italians who came from these regions to make Scotland their home.

The foot can be considered to be inspired (or re-invented) by the foot of Constantine in the Campidoglio in Rome. The hand, rather Egyptian, invites (as most social sculptures do) human intimacy.

In the spirit of the text men and women will rest in the shadow of the trees, watching their children play on the hand, or see, early in the morning, birds taking advantage of the pools collected on the palm of the hand.

TO LORENZA DEMARCO

From a letter to Lorenza Demarco, dated 13th April 1995

YOU WILL PROBABLY realise that I have already done some sculptures at St Mary's Cathedral at the top of Leith Walk. At the time, I did suggest that these objects could have been inscribed in the memory of the Italians who died on the SS Andora Star in 1940 … I am more than aware that this day in history should have an annual commemoration. It has always seemed to me strange that an annual mass was never said in connection with this tragic event. You are also possibly aware that making a statue as you suggest has bizarre political implications.

I wish you well in your enterprise and perhaps you can inform me of any progress that you might be able to make.

'The Artist as Hephaestus'
by permission of Frank Thurston

The sculptor's hand

Halla Bellof

THE SCULPTOR'S HAND is his instrument. His power is there. Paolozzi's hand has entered the public domain. Its is sold on post-cards at the National Galleries. It is sold on a mouse-mat in London. We can glide over it virtually, but intimately, continually.

The Snowdon close-up portrait of the hand shows it among stone fragments and we can see its finger-print whorls as well as its calluses. His unique and forensic identity is established.

At first glance it is the hand of an infant. It is so stubby. The joints are so close. Not for him the romantic long tapering finger. Here is a metaphor for his spirit and his art. It is rough and strong and stresses the earth and the grotesque whgich are in the beauty and vehemence of his figures.

He sees himself as Hephaestus, the ancestor of an artist of bronze. The vision is apt. In early life Hephaestus was despised, physically, and as an outsider. It was his great works which included the armour of Achilles which brought him his renown. As Robert Graves has it, he is ugly and ill-tempered but all his work is of matchless skill.

There is a whole series of Hephaestus figures but the original self-portrait as Hephaestus stands larger than life in Holborn, London. It is the only public statue, the only man, who stands on the pavement at our level, ready for us to touch, to stroke his hand. We know Paolozzi because we know his hand.

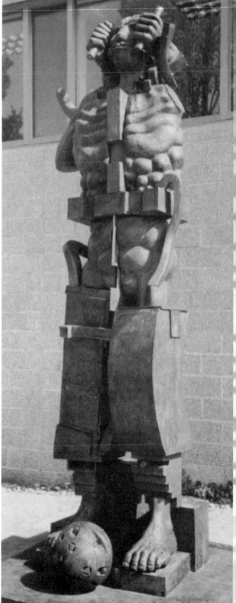

Paolozzi's figures

Duncan Macmillan

IN 1995, PROFESSOR David Finnegan, Director of the Institute of Cell and Molecular Biology at the University of Edinburgh, came to see me to say they were working on a project at King's Buildings (the university's science campus); the Swann Building, designed by Thomas Henney, Architects, and Ove Arup and Partners. As the new Institute of Cell and Molecular Biology, it was to be home to some of the most advanced investigations into the fundamental mechanics of life itself. Did I have any ideas for an artist who could provide something appropriate to decorate the building and symbolise the aspirations of this research? There seemed only one choice: Sir Eduardo Paolozzi.

There followed a meeting with Sir Eduardo and he responded to the idea with enthusiasm. Eventually a package was put together that made it possible to give him this commission. The last part was put in place with a grant of £26,000 from the Scottish Arts Council Lottery Fund. But Sir Eduardo's own generosity was a major factor in making the project possible.

But why should one artist stand out so clearly from all the rest when a commission like this was in question? A Royal Academician, the Queen's Sculptor in Scotland, was this not just ducking choice, taking the safe option with an establishment figure? Hardly: even at a very simple level of experience, few artists have worked on so many major public commissions. From the Festival of Britain to the British Library, over nearly fifty years

Eduardo Paolozzi has provided striking, original and wholly appropriate work in response to challenging and highly visible commissions. But this is not, nor has ever been, because he has been willing to compromise and provide comfortable and undemanding work. The sculpture he has produced in response to commissions in Edinburgh, London, Munich and many other places throughout the world has always been original, thought provoking and also truly monumental in a way that is unusual in modern sculpture.

Paolozzi was born in Edinburgh and trained briefly here before leaving first for London and then Paris where he stayed from 1947-1949. His art really has its origins in the inspiration that he derived then from the Surrealists and Dadaists, figures like Giacometti, Duchamp, Max Ernst and Tristan Tzara, some of whom he met in Paris at that time. Two perceptions are already reflected in it at this early date, and whatever the inspiration that fed them, they were both wholly original. But, in addition, neither is peculiar in some way to the province of art, nor is it some quirky, personal notion. Instead both reflect on the whole field of our intellectual and imaginative experience and the ways in which we structure it, and both seem to be visible in almost everything he has done since then.

One is that in the huge range of imagery that we deal with day to day, right across the board from comic books through the news media to the sciences, art can claim no special privilege. These images, however grand or however humble, are all reflections on the modern world, our place in it and the way we understand it. And between them — as they have always done — they enshrine the icons around which we construct our imaginative and spiritual lives. Now, just as ten thousand years ago, these are not the product of some special separate activity called art. They are a reflection of the way we live. They fulfil a primitive need that has not changed. This means that the primitive itself is not a state. It is part of us It is only the way we see ourselves that that distances us from others' less technologically advanced cultures. We think we are different, but we are not and share out fundamental needs with all mankind.

The other perception that underlies Paolozzi's art is that the surrealist technique of collage — cutting things up and reassembling them to create a wholly new, compound identity — is as close as we can get to reflecting the extraordinary flux of intercutting ideas, images and perceptions that constitute the reality of our daily lives.

These two ideas came together in a highly unorthodox, dramatic lecture that Paolozzi gave to the ICA in London in 1952. It was one of the key moments in the development of Pop-art, but he himself moved quickly beyond it developing these ideas into a rich and complex art that was quite his own.

He has worked since then as a sculptor and as a print maker, and in other fields of the applied arts, and he has explored many themes. One which has always been central to his art though has been the vision of humanity and the imaginative goals that we pursue, in our lives, whether consciously or unconsciously, in the technologically dominated world in which we live. Thus the elision, through collage, of the scientific or technological with the ordinarily human has been a constant in his work since the late forties, even as it has evolved continuously since then.

His ideas developed dramatically even in the time that elapsed between the first discussions over the Swann Building commission and the completion of the two sculptures. Indeed these continued to evolve until they were actually in place. The result is that they are monumental, but also improvised; provisional, like all thought. They are cast in bronze, yet seem ready to shift, change, rearrange themselves from moment to moment. That is the way Paolozzi works, reflecting as he does so, the way in which we think.

In the evolution of this commission, from the start, he proposed a work based on two or more standing figures that would stand outside the building, but even as they stood, would interact with each other. The figures that he provided in the final work are twice life-size. They stand ten feet high, truly monumental. But they are not simple standing figures, static like the kings, generals, and politicians who make up the bulk of monumental public sculpture in our city streets and squares. Instead they are energetic. Sited by the door of the building, they are like the fierce guardians of the Buddhist temples of China and Japan. But they are characteristic Paolozzi figures too, a compound of human, mechanical, and geometric elements, cast separately, assembled it seems almost arbitrarily, and yet struggling into life, just as Michelangelo's unfinished Slaves seem to struggle against the incoherent burden of the uncut stone from which they are formed.

Paolozzi's figures represent the scattered pieces of the jig-saw of under-standing made coherent by the power of the imagination. They go back to a standing figure he made some years ago, the figure of Hephaestos, limping artificer to the gods on Olympus, model of the modern scientist in his boundless ingenuity, but frail and human too. The role of the imagination in the astonishing feats of science is symbolised in them, but so too is the vulnerable, organic life which is the subject of study in the Swann Building. It is appropriate that they should guard it as they do. But there is also something else strikingly appropriate about them.

From the start they were conceived as tumblers, and so, fittingly for public art, as street performers. In a series of maquettes he pursued this idea: acrobats doing somersaults and handstands, performing; displaying feats of skill that few of us can emulate. As they are finally installed, one is standing upright, the other on its head. They are a kind of perpetual street theatre to entertain the people working at King's Buildings, and they are sited so as to be visible from several directions. They are street theatre, but they are also profoundly serious. In the way they are made, they pose the question: What happens when you take life apart and put it together again? Dr. Frankenstein is never far away.

Indeed the left hand figure, standing with fists clutched to its brow, takes this essential detail from a figure drawn by William Blake of Cain running from the murdered body of his brother Abel. Cain the farmer murdered Abel the shepherd. Cain represented progress, technical progress from pastoral to agrarian, from the passive to the active relationship with the natural world, the relationship on which science depends. We are Cain's heirs, but at what cost? It is right to ask such questions in a context like this.

Paolozzi has worked all his life to construct a vision that accommodates the profound changes wrought by science and technology and their implications for humanity. But he has not simply looked in awe at the achievements of science. Nor has he condemned it and its impact on human life. He has kept in view the fact that science itself is the product of human aspiration powered by the imagination: that what is needed, therefore, in the face of its achievements, is a vision of humanity that can reconcile it with all the other human needs, imaginative and spiritual as well as material, which may have been obscured, but have not been made redundant by the technological lives we lead.

When the King's Buildings campus was begun at the end of the 1920s, this notion was evidently not so strange. In the tradition of the Arts and Crafts movement and its commitment to public art all the first buildings there were decorated with sculpture, with works of the imagination. Sir Robert Lorimer's Zoology Building, for instance, has a magnificent series of animal reliefs on it by Phyllis Bone. Together the decoration of these buildings probably constituted the largest group of works of art ever commissioned by the University. Since that brave beginning however, there has not been much. The occasional Principal commemorated in a portrait, but nothing else. Art was seen as a luxury, but it is not.

And a few years ago, Paolozzi put on an exhibition in the Museum of Mankind that argued why this it is not. He called it Lost Magic Kingdoms. It was an important statement of something central to his art and to our lives. It was selected from the Museum's great ethnological collections, but he added work of his own and things that he had collected, products of modern culture.

The point of the title was twofold. It expressed regret at the loss of so many of the cultures represented in the Museum's collections, but also how in our own culture, we have lost sight of these magic kingdoms of the mind. We too need the life of the spirit and the imagination that resides in them. We need our totems and our taboos and we have them too, just as much if we are scientists as if we are artists, though we do not always recognise them for what they are. And because our sensibility is so fractured, it needs a unique, comprehensive vision to forge something that can hold the parts together in a single image. That is what we have here.

The result is peculiarly appropriate to the Swann Building and its function, but the sculpture also provides a symbol for the whole King's Buildings campus. This is how David Hume put it: "Tis evident that all the sciences have a relation, greater or less, to human nature; and that, however wide any of them may seem to run from it, they still return back by one passage or another.'

These figures, and the ambition they enshrine, belong in a long development in Sir Eduardo's art. Early in his career he produced a remarkable series of machine men. Mechanical monsters, inhuman deities for a dehumanised technological world, they could have stepped out of Fritz Lang's *Metropolis*. This theme continued right through the seventies, but it was not simply pessimistic and fifteen years or so ago, he started to look again at the classical tradition of the human figure shaped by the ideal. He turned especially to the great hieratic figures of archaic Greece, but sought to reconstruct them out of the fragmented, compound vision of modern life. From there his inspiration moved to Rodin who saw how the fragment, that had always been so important to Paolozzi, was actually at the centre of the way in which we know the classical tradition. We know it from the fragments of ancient literature, the bits of antique sculpture, the ruins of classical architecture. Even so we managed to create the Renaissance in part at least from such inspiration, and so it is a model of all knowledge, pieced together as that is from all the disparate fragments of our experience fused together by the imagination.

This inspiration has produced a remarkable series of works. Not counting the works at the Dean Gallery, or the great standing figure of Vulcan installed there, in the streets of Edinburgh there are two other major public sculptures by Paolozzi which reflect it. Near his birthplace in Leith Walk, there is 'The Manuscript of Monte Cassino,' a soliloquy on the whole theme of the humanist civilisation that derives from the classical tradition, its present state, its past and its future. It was of course this tradition that inspired Edinburgh's New Town on the edge of which the sculpture is sited.

Then for the Royal Bank of Scotland at South Gyle, Paolozzi built 'The Wealth of Nations,' some five metres high, a gigantic, fragmented figure struggling into life, or a fallen giant, a permanent reminder to the Bank that the true wealth of nations lies, not in cash or coin. Nor can it be described on any balance sheet. It lies beyond calculation in the human gifts of sympathy, creativity and invention, powered by the imagination.

Like the Swann building sculptures and 'The Manuscript of Monte Cassino', 'The Wealth of Nations' is an image made up of parts of a human figure. Indeed at first sight it looks like some enormous, disassembled fallen giant, some tumbled Colossus, crumbled relic of a once mighty civilisation now forgotten. But the head is for thought, the hands are for action and the feet are for movement and here the huge feet are indeed poised to move. There is energy in the grip of the hands and the head is not blank or passive, but, already raised above the ground, it seems about to sit up and take notice. These human features are also joined by curving abstract elements, their lines tense as springs and full of energy. This is not a ruined memorial to some long forgotten folie-de-grandeur, therefore, but a new giant emerging, struggling out of chaos, reforming itself, rediscovering by its energy and effort of will the possibility of articulated action. And of course this mighty figure does not belong to another civilisation at all, but

exclusively to our own. It is not retrospective, a relic of the past, but a challenge to the future, our future. Its struggle reflects the struggle we must all engage in to preserve our essential humanity in an increasingly depersonalised technological world.

It was the great thinkers of the Scottish Enlightenment, David Hume and Adam Smith, who recognised that the key to that humanity is the imagination. It not only makes it possible to order knowledge, but, as Adam Smith argued in his other great book, *The Theory of Moral Sentiments*, as sympathy, the imaginative projection of one mind into the feelings of another, imagination is the cement that holds society together.

It is also precisely as a reflection of these fundamental insights of the Enlightenment that throughout his long career the key to Paolozzi's art has been his use of the surrealist technique of collage. It is the imagination which produces the new compound identities of his reassembled figures, just as it unifies the flux of ideas, feelings, images and perceptions that constitute the fractured reality we live through, and transforms it into the continuing flow of individual consciousness. On the base of 'The Wealth of Nations' Paolozzi summarises all this, and so indirectly describes his own work, in Einstein's words inscribed there: 'Knowledge is wonderful, but imagination is even better.' It is indeed imagination that puts knowledge to human use, binds together the scattered pieces of the jig-saw of understanding and makes them coherent. These works remind us of an essential truth, therefore; the order we live by is not rational, but imaginative. They are public works, not by their location alone, nor simply because of their scale, but in the true meaning of the word because they state a fundamental truth whose meaning belongs to us collectively as a society.

DUNCAN MACMILLAN is Curator of the Talbot Rice Gallery, at the University of Edinburgh

Notes from a
Paolozzi Piazza

Richard Price

The skull's a casing.
Look at a gasket —
it's an inkblot
and now you're making connections.

Inside the sealed unit
an engine block swivels
on the elbow of a pair of calipers,
body implied.

Paolozzi, you're underground
and as popular
as public transport.

From Tube Shelter Perspective, 1993

WHEN I WROTE that poem, I had been living in London only a short while. It felt at the time that you could not go far in London without seeing a Paolozzi sculpture, and that a meditation on or even agressive occupation of city space was itself part of his aesthetic. By road, rail, or underground you would see his work before very long. If you missed perhaps my favourite work of his, the understated yet large lumplike structure, topped with a little city (or *is* it an engine casing?) in the scruffy grounds in front of Euston Station, then soon enough you'd come across his vivid, even garish, tiles at the underground station in Tottenham Court Road. Or, from the top of a bus, you'd maybe see his lacerated giant, *The Artist as Hephaestus*, on High Holborn. And so on…

Paolozzi was in that sense a very public artist (since then, the number of 'Paolozzis' in London has increased), and that last verse was intended to capture a number of ambiguities about very public art. Paolozzi has managed to use what might at one time have seemed avant-garde (or 'underground') practices but he is also accepted by committee-land as an exemplary and therefore reassuring artist. Paolozzi's work is popular in the sense that many people see it, have to see it, just like they may have to use a bus or a train; that does not guarantee 'popularity' in the normal sense of the word, though. Whether or not Paolozzi is indeed popular in that sense, too, is not really the point here; I am also unable to answer it and I would question the poll that proved it one way or the other. Paolozzi's sculptures are imposed on those who will experience them most, whether or not they wish it, even though they clearly have something 'representational' to say, apparently representational even of the people who are most likely to come into contact with the work. The three-way conflict between the artist's individuality and vision, the wishes of the often second-guessing commissioning authority, and 'the public' themselves, is brought into its starkest relief with public art of this kind.

Paolozzi's work in London seems to me to have a sentinel role. In that sense, and in the similar if cruder combination of man and machine in theme and form, Antony Gormley's *Angel of the North,* may owe a good deal to the elder sculptor. The northern Angel is famously visible from the road (and, less dramatically, from passing trains). It reminds you maybe of the inscrutable single standing stones which could be funeral masonry or boundary sculpture, or both. At the same time as it is a territory marker it is a homage to the largely defunct heavy industries of the land it both guards and acts as ambassador to. The Angel is therefore, in one sense, the final nail in the coffin for one kind of 'North' (the question of its appearing to be an all too serene crucifixion of religion itself, a sleepwalking angel painlessly put to death on an old plane's wing, I shall leave for another time). Like George Wyllie's straw train suspended from Glasgow's Finnieston

Crane, though with less anger, Gormley's work attempts to 'finish' a constituted period in a partially self-identifying culture's history. The last nail in the coffin might also be the first nail of another, perhaps brighter, but certainly different structure — if, courtesy of one of the paradoxes of cultural symbolism, self-confidence can be successfully encouraged by a monument to failure.

I've already hinted at my doubts about the mildness of Gormley's aesthetic. I find Gormley's work nostalgic in a way that Paolozzi seldom is. (I enjoy this nostalgia to begin with, but guilt crops up the morning after, or sooner). For one thing, Paolozzi seems to remain interested in new technological process and structure, though his sculptures can look a bit 1950s Forbidden Planet; for another, there are literal faultlines in his human figures which can be read as physically realised doubts about both industrial progress and / or humankind's own special status as in control of self. I think I am sharing something with Paolozzi in the poems concerned with sculpture in my own work. Especially in *Renfrewshire in Old Photographs,* where my concerns have a great deal to do with the representational qualities of the plastic arts in the landscape, I have tried to evoke, among other things, a more violent relationship with the industrial past, a remembrance of human cost. In 'On Barochan Hill,' for instance, in which a scrapyard Hillman Avenger is imagined to be installed on a hill previously set aside for a Celtic cross, I have tried to eschew passivity, to channel and approach a public representation of anger, pure and not so simple. Even the half-buried rhyme and wraparound rhythm is meant to evoke crumple at speed:

When we raise a new cross on Barochan Hill
it will not be a Cross. To serve us instead
we'll haul up a wreck from Linwood's old works,
pull a car out a Renfrew scrappy.

Imagine the pulleys, the drive up the field,
the event. We'll rub its nose in the plinth, force
all its doors aghast. We'll build to last that dive
only ad cars pull themselves out of.

(from Renfrewshire in Old Photographs, 2000)

Obviously, the relationship between humans and mechanisation is one of Paolozzi's major themes. Yet — and while still avoiding what I find to be Gormley's awkward softnesses — the histrionics of the voice I've tried to ventriloquize in the poem above are not part of Paolozzi's world at all. You might find the odd combination of bright and dirty cream tiles in Tottenham Court Road a kind of deliberate tastelessness, but even its harking back (if I read it rightly) to the mosaics of Crete is as much chirpy as anything else. Unlike the tiles, an engagement with the horror and sexual brute force of the Labyrinth, has not been laid on with a trowel. You might find that the square-ish elements in Paolozzi's portrait of Count Basie or of Richard Rogers, or any of the other (perhaps rather repetitive) Paolozzi heads, are suggestive of satire, but that would be a profound misreading of figures Paolozzi admires. Perhaps the smoothest, least fractured of Paolozzi's heads is entitled 'The Critic.'

Nevertheless, like Gormley, and like my imaginary installation, key public sculptures by Paolozzi are 'stationed'. The Euston sculpture, for example, marks the threshold to the whole of the city to anyone leaving Euston by that southwest path. Bewildered travellers from the north might come across it and even take solace in its vision of even the city being dwarfed by the vast, deep, Earth on which it rests. London, it seems to say, is only a speck in the grand scheme of things (I don't know why, but a reminder of *everyone's* anonymity on a universal scale always cheers me up). The city is a *connected speck* — and the Earth is a kind of engine casing, too — but it is a speck all the same.

East-coast Scots thinking they can escape going through London without seeing a Paolozzi may be thwarted if, after leaving King's Cross and heading up the Euston Road, they glance north. They will then find Paolozzi's large sculpture of a bethroned but crouching Isaac Newton, based on Blake's satirical print, just visible through the grid gates of the British Library. Ever since this vast squatting figure — artists working in England in the last twenty years seem to have re-engaged themselves with the ancient landscape art of Cerne Abbas — was installed there has been debate about its meaning. It still draws the question just now and again as to why a Library which is in truth the leading combined resource for both science and humanities research in Europe should adopt as its guardian statue a figure who is at the receiving end of Blake's most biased disdain. The original print, after all, shows the 'blindness' of one of the world's greatest scientists, picturing Newton oblivious to the undersea world he sits within as he divides the universe with his pair of compasses. A simple answer is that Blake may well have meant Newton's worldview harm, but Paolozzi and the builders of a public service and public-spirited infrastructure certainly don't. Paolozzi, as I read it, is not paying a tribute to Blake, he is putting him right. Blake, the sculpture seems to say, was as much guilty of separating the mathematical world from the sensual and psychological one as ever Newton was. The bolts and angularities of Paolozzi's new work offer a synthesis of kind that Blake might well have lamented, but which is nevertheless, in one sense, of the nature of a Blakean unity (without the ecstasy, and, naively I think, without the agony).

The Paolozzi Newton, like other full-height bodies by him, also reminds me of the proportions of a baby or small infant — the head in particular seems just a little too big. Even the single heads seem simplifed, cartoonised, to me. Perhaps that is where there is some bite to his work.

After all, what is Paolozzi saying to us if his figurative sculpture constitutes a workforce of calm, infantile robots?

RICHARD PRICE'S books include the poetry collections *Perfume & Petrol Fumes* (Diehard: 1999) and *Hand Held* (Akros: 1997). Most recently he has co-edited with David Kinloch *La Nouvelle Alliance: Influences francophones sur la littérature écossaise moderne* (ELLUG: 2000).

Impressions: of Eduardo Paolozzi

A.J.P. Thomson

THERE ARE A number of recurrent difficulties in writing about art, and in particular in negotiating between the twin peaks of technique and of theme. How are we to relate form and content? Hegel's famous account of art, as that through which spirit manifests itself, relies on this apparently inescapable division between that which is represented and the mode of its representation. Yet the consequences of this position are deeply ambivalent. On the one hand, if we focus too heavily on the meaning of art, on what is portrayed by it or in it, we run the risk of reducing the work of art to being merely an obstacle, something to be overcome, or at worst, a falsification of the world. On the other hand, too much emphasis on the artwork in itself leads us to reduce all art to an insular aestheticism, which refuses to connect with the world. The traditional resort of criticism is to some kind of historical taxonomy. Indeed, as Rodolphe Gasché has argued, the development of art history is a model for the development of all aesthetic and historical studies.

The consequences are plain for students of Paolozzi's work. How to account for Paolozzi's originality? Either the artist must be assigned a place in the history of art — and often the deeply misleading title of Pop Artist — or analysed in terms of his influences or sources. In both cases the same ambiguity returns: how to talk about the work without reducing it to a aesthetic-historical artefact (symptom of an era, an art movement) or the repetition of other motifs and works. Can the singularity of a work of art be measured in terms of similarity or difference from another work or group of works, without missing precisely that in the work of it which is distinctive, which makes it utterly unlike the point of comparison?

These are both problems of mimesis. In the first instance thinking the relationship between artwork and world has been and remains massively dominated by the concept of mimesis — of imitation. The work of art both portrays and betrays its subject; it can be seen as a bad fiction, a poor imitation from one point of view, but the same tradition also prescribes art's role in conveying an essence or truth of the world, of experience, which would otherwise escape. For the second example, the problem of mimesis is inserted into the question of the originality of the artist's work.

In attempting to characterise the art of Eduardo Paolozzi, I am aware that the methodological problems will not go away; indeed, that they may be inescapable. However I have deliberately set out with several intentions in mind: to read Paolozzi's works without relying on his place in a list of other artists; to find a way to establish the common-ground between the apparent themes of his works with their artistic expression; and perhaps to work towards the limits of the problems I have posed, as issues of mimesis.

I take my bearings and my title for this essay from a relatively free translation of Philippe Lacoue-Labarthe's 'Typography.' In adapting his 'typography' to my 'impressions' I hope to show not only a continuity of concerns between Lacoue-Labarthe's thought and the work of Eduardo Paolozzi, but also to characterise Paolozzi's art in such a way as to reveal its most political aspects. But at the same time, I wish to mark out my own position as one of a certain discursive modesty — to remind the reader that these are *only* impressions, and only my impressions.

For Lacoue-Labarthe the term 'typography' is the title not only of an essay, but a heading for his work as a whole, since two of his books, *Le sujet de la philosophie* and *L'imitation des modernes*, are subtitled *Typographies I* and *II*. In his more well known *La fiction du politique*, translated as *Heidegger, Art and Politics*, he insists that he is continuing the same trajectory mapped out in the early essay. Under this heading, his aim is to rethink the relationship between politics and mimesis in the Western tradition, from Plato to Heidegger.

I read this as an attempt to effect a shift in ontology from thinking in terms of singularities, of unique individuals or events, to thinking in terms of types, of figures. The objective would be to think mimesis not in terms of a model and a copy, but in terms of a series of copies without an original, an ideal. In philosophical terms this is contiguous with the re-reading of Heidegger by Derrida and others; it can also been seen to re-enact the questions of certain forms of modernist literature, including the Surrealists and Mallarmé, as to the efficacy of representational thinking and writing.

At stake are the questions of mimesis, of technology, and of politics, none of which can ever be said to have been far from Paolozzi's work. On one side lies his inheritance from the Surrealists; on the other his concern to reflect and respond to the practices of everyday life in the technological age.

It is not just this stamp in which I am interested, but the convergence of the move from thinking of art in terms of the individual romantic genius, who somehow synthesises and distils the symbol which connects the material world to that of ideas, with the idea of the present age as technological. The stamp, the impression, would be the appropriate artistic form for such an age as it would raise most forcefully the twin problems of political agency, and the remains of the human within technology.

From his early practice of pressing found objects — cogs, scrap metal, the cast-offs of other works — into his sculptures, Paolozzi has developed a whole visual vocabulary of impressions; and an array of techniques to translate his concerns from one medium to another. This is evident not only in his figural sculptures, in which whole armies of battered robots and knocked-about cyborgs lurch around, but also in his insistent return to the human figure and the head in particular, in drawings, prints and collages, from the 1950s to the 1990s. The figure is always to be considered against the background of the technical process which makes our representation of it possible, pointing up technology as the distinctive horizon of our era.

The paradox of touch — that we cannot touch something without in turn being touched by it — is operative throughout these impressions. Which would imply that we might not be able to tell the difference between an artwork that had been touched, marked or moulded by technology, and one that touches it back, critiques or challenges it. More generally, is the human that which tempers and moderates the machine, or is our only experience of technology to be that of its domination over nature?

Paolozzi's insistent attempts to locate political images within this space of questioning have often been neglected by his interpreters. But can we fail to notice the recurrent military images in his screenprints and collages? Isn't Paolozzi's visual imagination as driven by the circulation of the representation of violence as it is by B-movie monsters and science fiction? But even more telling, is his relocation of the problem of politics at the level of form. Behind the post-war externalisation of fear in popular culture into aliens and robots lies the experience of the Second World War itself.

Lacoue-Labarthe suggests that Nazism is the fatal culmination of a way of thinking about politics which models itself on mimesis, and which seeks to mould a state to an ideal, by the forceful exclusion of that which does not fit its self-image. The attempt to break with mimesis, so powerful for nearly a century of avant-garde artists, is thus an attempt to break with a political thinking which organises the state around a logic of imitation which holds within it an ideal.

We can clarify this by considering technology. Either we can understand technology as both the symptom and the great symbol of mankind's rise and fall, of the achievements bought at the price of domination over nature, of the possibility both of catastrophic violence and slow destruction of the planet by the excessive economies of the West. In which case we can try and conceal ourselves in the cosy nostalgia for a past before technology, a pre-modern or pre-industrial age. But this is a logic of history which restores mimesis in one of its most powerful forms, as the myth of a Golden Age, of which the present is but a pale imitation.

But what if there were another way of thinking about technology, and about history? One which didn't seek to escape, or to turn our fascinated gaze away from the present? This might be the thought of a technological age with no outside, with no imaginable end. So Paolozzi's figures and heads are not the signs of a degeneration of the human, but a more sophisticated understanding that to forget the machine within the human is to deny responsibility for the effects of global technology.

If we cannot work outside the paradigms of mimesis, this way of thinking might have to be only a thought of impressions; but I will propose how we might extend it beyond the cybernetics of Paolozzi's sculptures. So, for a start, there is his extensive work with relief. Most famously in Scotland there are the doors for the Hunterian Gallery in Glasgow, and the ceiling panels which were originally designed for Cleish Castle, but which can now be found in the Dean Gallery. Relief work seems a natural extension of the principle of impressions; the two dimensional surface becomes moulded and distended. The interaction with the screenprints and drawings of the 1970s is also clear, as the same shapes recur: elongated blocks of colour in the prints replaced with blocks of varying depth, and thus varying proportions of light and shadow, in the reliefs. (What happens if we rethink sculpture in terms of surfaces rather than volumes?)

The techniques of impression generate both a method of drawing with shade, and a way of sculpting in two dimensions: several of the prints, in their turn, seem to acquire depth, as if there were grooves impressed into the paper itself. Taken to its natural extension, this same impulse has seen Paolozzi work with relief prints and become interested in shaping paper itself. At the Munich Academy of Fine Arts he had papermaking equipment installed; the impetus, and the funding, coming from Eduardo himself, according to Dr Rudolf Seitz, President of the Academy in Robin Spencer's *Recurring Themes* catalogue.

The artist's creative response to the problems posed by a public sculpture at Mönchengladbach exemplify these principles. As described in Frank Whitford's *Eduardo Paolozzi: Private Vision, Public Art*, a restricted budget prevented Paolozzi from constructing the three dimensional relief he had originally proposed. Instead, the final work etched the pattern onto the wall in strips of stainless steel. The belts of steel project out from the wall, and as the light catches them, the shadows they cast throw an ever-changing sketch across the wall. The work hovers between two and three dimensions, since the three-dimensional elements function alternately as lines and as volumes. Or we might think instead of the thousands of mosaic tiles, impressed into their ground, at Tottenham Court Road Tube station and at Kingfisher Shopping Centre in Redditch. Here too, Paolozzi is drawing with thousands of tiny objects, while sculpting a three-dimensional form from tiny coloured surfaces. No substantial difference, perhaps, from his pages and pages of scrapbook collages, as visual detritus is accumulated in layers to produce an image which depends on its depth as much as on its.

When these scrapbooks come to be transposed into the fantastic series of screen-prints that the artist undertook with Kelpra studios in the late sixties and early seventies, the principle of impression is extended further. What is fascinating about the screenprinting process is not only the layering of ink which can give not only depth but texture to an apparently flat image, but also the distance between the artist's hand and the print as it is produced. Working towards a print is always to work at one remove;

whether preparing a screen, a lithographic stone or an etching plate. The family resemblance between printing processes lies in is this alienation of creator from created. Where this has often been seen a sign of the medium's retrograde status, does it not instead point out something more essential than the intimate connection of artist's soul to the spirit of the work? There must always remain an element of chance in the transposition from artist's positive to the negative from which the final image is to be drawn. Printmaking will always be a matter of impressions.

Nor should we forget that when Paolozzi began to work with offset lithographic techniques, he is engaged in the blurring of distinctions between art as product and art as icon; between the commercial and the fine art processes of production. Or, to return to Lacoue-Labarthe and our discussion of type itself, the question of mass reproduction; against which the unique art-work has had to define itself since before the invention of photography. How to tell the difference between a genuine print and a copy? And now, when colour photocopying, desktop scanners and cheap printing technology has made reproduction almost ubiquitous? Don't tell me it's just a question of an impression…

So with Paolozzi's art, we are located beyond the romantic paradigm of the artist, whose mission is the education of the nation into its foundational myths, and whose role revolves around the creation of unique and iconic works. Paolozzi's very own impression-ism is the dislocation of this traditional logic of what constitutes *culture* itself. Instead of the sculptor of clay, who draws his materials from the soil, and whose spirit must be instilled into the blood of the nation, doesn't Paolozzi recast the sculptor with the oil-soaked hands of the engineer, or the sweat-soaked palms of the machinist? Or even as the type-writer (typo-graphist?) itself?

Paolozzi's writings

Robin Spencer

Key phrases, like key sculpture, takes time to make. The arrival at a plastic iconography is just as difficult as a language. A few sculptures per year can alter other plastic values. A few key statements can have a similar effect.

Eduardo Paolozzi, 'Notes from a lecture at the Institute of Contemporary Arts, 1951', *Uppercase No.1, 1958*

THE VISUAL EXPRESSION of the word, as both idea and experience which could be apprehended simultaneously, was Mallarmé's legacy of the *Coup de Dés* to the modernists of the last century; from Apollinaire's calligrammes, Picasso's collages and Futurist writing to the wooden shapes Arp made according to the laws of chance which were shaped like sentences, and the collages and word poems of Schwitters to which were later added sounds. Paolozzi would count several of these great modernists from the last century who also wrote poetry and prose as influences on his own art and writing. He has also noted in respect of Arp, that when he was asked whether he preferred to be remembered for his writing or his art he replied that he would choose the former. Everything in the world, which Mallarmé once remarked, ends up in a book, will eventually be redistributed in cyberspace.

With Jean Arp, first called Hans, who was born in Strasbourg and spoke three languages, Paolozzi shared a similar linguistic facility when he grew up in Edinburgh between the wars. He could switch automatically from English to Italian, and speak in two dialects. His childhood years, in the decade after the linguist Saussure and the philosopher Wittgenstein, whose life and work Paolozzi commemorated when he was forty years old, were the decades of surrealism, which began as a literary movement, and to which he has been attracted all his working life. Speaking of the significance of surrealism for him, he has emphasised how important it is 'not to have a feeling of frontiers between the various arts.' In the same years there was also Amédée Ozenfant's book *Foundations of Modern Art* (1928) which used word and image to juxtapose the ancient with the modern, nature with science, the European with the 'primitive.' Paolozzi found Ozenfant's book while he was serving as a soldier in the Pioneer Corps in 1943, when he had time on his hands to contemplate the débacle of 1939 and what might ultimately emerge from it. Since then, Paolozzi has spent more than half a century of his art reconciling that sense of pre-war optimism which he experienced as a child in Edinburgh — of what might have been had Europe not been so decisively diverted from its course — with the reality of what came afterwards, by examining in sculpture and prints those modern mythologies of post-war experience which include: relationships between nature and the man-made world, and between war and peace; images of technology, with their aura of outmoded obsolescence; the grotesque and the uncanny as repressions of cultural anxiety; and representations of pleasure which a society makes to mask its collective pain.

As a student at the Slade School in the last year of the war, he came into contact with surrealist art and literature through Roland Penrose and others, including the Belgian surrealist E.L.T. Mesens who ran the London Gallery. Surrealism was powerful, Paolozzi has said, 'because it embraced several art forms and mediums, including waiting and the cinema; and gave expression to experiences such as black humour and eroticism which other art could not.' He read David Gascoyne's translation of André Breton's *What is Surrealism?* (1936), which was a decisive influence on him, leaving for Paris in the summer of 1947, never intending to return to England.

In Paris between 1947 and 1949 Paolozzi browsed in the bouquinistes of the Seine and St Germain-des-Prés with the Dadaist poet Tristan Tzara in whose apartment he remembers seeing fading collages by Picasso, African sculpture and Tzara's collection of *livres de luxe*. The revaluation of the commonplace by the surrealists, and existentialists such as Francis Ponge — whose poems *Le Partis pris des choses* (1941), transform the most ordinary objects, even a pebble, into the marvellous — has continued to inspire Paolozzi, whose intention is still to 'begin a work with something banal and end up with something poetic.' In Paris he was also often in the company of Alberto Glacometti and Balthus, and remembers them talking about English literature. On one occasion Balthus asked him to bring back a copy of Dickens's last, unfinished, novel *Edwin Drood* when he was next in London. Paolozzi has told me that Giacometti always spoke to him in his native Swiss Italian; whereas with others outside his family, Giacometti only ever spoke French, which Paolozzi's friend, the English sculptor Raymond Mason can confirm. Paolozzi read Louis Aragon's *Le Paysan de Paris* (1924) and Raymond Roussel's *Impressions d'Afrique* (1910). Roussel's strangely contrived mechanical world, which had inspired Duchamp thirty-five years before, gave Paolozzi the idea of writing a pastiche novel based on it; shortly afterwards he found the same author's *Comment j'ai écrit certain de mes livres* (1935). Within a decade Roussel's writing methods had became an important influence on his own.

The *bricolage* of everyday experience and its imagery, including the cinema, American pulp magazines and science fiction, which Paolozzi pioneered as a member of the Independent Group in the early 1950s, was accompanied by a rejection of the worn-out values associated with the conventions of English literature as well as art; and an acknowledgement of the expressive power of language. In a lecture about his own work given at the ICA in 1958 he said, 'It is conceivable that in 1958 a higher order of imagination exists in a SF pulp produced on the outskirts of LA than in the little magazines of today.'

The written word as a weapon
The word written is to weep
Cry out a language
Sea Light Sun Wheel
Electric Sculpture
The magic Japanese Water language

Between 1960 and 1962 Paolozzi was Visiting Professor in Hamburg where he taught a course on surrealism which he called 'The Translation of Experience' (the same title, incidentally, used for master classes in Salzburg in the summer of 1981, and again in Edinburgh as recently as 1997). Ready-made material, much of it damaged and pre-war, including illustrated books, was obtained from a large second-hand book shop in Hamburg, for his students to make collages and poetry. Some of this material was used for Paolozzi's 48 page screenprinted book *Metafisikal Translations* (1962) — published by Christopher Prater's Kelpra Studio, with whom he had recently begun to make screenprints — and for the twelve minute film *The History of Nothing* (1962) which Paolozzi has described as 'a homage to Surrealism.' The random juxtaposition of the collaged elements in both book and film (which includes a soundtrack of music and other sounds recorded at different speeds), provided another outlet for exploring the relationships between word and image which he was then developing across several media, including the aluminium sculptures which were improvised with the help of a technician on the shop floor of an engineering works. The relationship between order and chance, as in Roussel, and its expression as sound, characterises Paolozzi's writings of the early 1960s. An additional source in Hamburg was the recently published *Scribbledehobble* (1961), the workbook which James Joyce used to 'harvest' words for *Finnegan's Wake*, a copy of which he gave to each of his twelve Hamburg students. For Stephen Spender, Paolozzi's poems gave him 'a lot to think about'; and in November 1961 he wanted to publish them in *Encounter.*

In 1964, Paolozzi told his fellow artist Richard Hamilton, 'Some people need, perhaps, [Clement] Greenberg, I need Wittgenstein.' By choosing captions for his twelve-print series *As Is When* from Wittgenstein's propositions, and showing several key events in the philosopher's life which he identified with, Paolozzi illustrated the thesis which Wittgenstein came to question towards the end of *The Tractatus Logico-Philosophicus* (1921), that language represents the world by depicting it. Wittgenstein 'picture' theory of language, and his subsequent development of 'language games' in the more mystical *Philosophical Investigations,* in which language is expressive of wider social and cultural realities and helps to explain its uses and meanings, suggested to Paolozzi that he could also treat words and language in the same way that he used objects and images to make sculpture and prints. For *As Is When* he provided an introduction sheet *Wild Track for Ludwig The Kakafon Kakkoon laka oon Elektrik Lafs*, which was put together from found texts. Although the material and effect is different, the process was similar to William Burroughs's 'cut-ups' for his novels of this period, such as *Nova Express* (1964). Paolozzi subsequently used words and their syntax for collage as he did with other material for his art. Words exist as given, or as found elements in the world, like objects and images which can be changed into something else or used for different purposes. Words can be reproduced and multiplied, split up and reduced, recombined and remade, and given a new meaning. With the book *Kex* (1966) (the name of a Swedish candy bar) Richard Hamilton was asked to edit the words and pictures which Paolozzi gave him in any relationship or order he liked. The intention, like the engineering aesthetic of the sculpture which maximised chance and distanced authorship, was to go beyond what Duchamp had done with the ready-mades, and recognize total experience by evolving, Paolozzi told Hamilton in 1965, 'a system on one's own beyond that result.' By the subsequent reproductive processes of printing, the material could be returned to its original form, which is either seen, as with a picture, or read, as in a book. The role of words and pictures can therefore be reversed, for their function depends on the form in which they ultimately end up, as in *Moonstrips Empire News* (1967) which consists of 100 screenprinted sheets. Forty of the sheets consist of found texts in different colours, several in semi-calligramatic form, and eighteen combine both texts and images. For the 'Viewer,' words stand in for pictures, while for the 'reader,' pictures can function as words.

General Dynamic FUN (1970), which consists of 50 screenprints and photolithographs, is the second part of *Moonstrips Empire News,* and has an introduction by the novelist J.G. Ballard, whose contribution to science fiction, once considered a 'marginal' genre of literature, is analogous with Paolozzi's revaluation of popular culture for fine art. Paolozzi's scepticism about the cultural reality of America — he was a regular visitor in the 1960s including a term as Visiting Professor of Sculpture at Berkeley in 1968 which he cut short — is also reflected in Ballard's powerful apocalyptic vision of the American Dream. In the 1960s they shared the automobile and crash across the media of sculpture, prints and novels, but unlike the deadpan delivery of disaster subjects by their American counterpart Andy Warhol, theirs was a more visceral response to the globalizing iconography of Americana interpreted from a critical European perspective which was then dominated by Vietnam. There are also similarities between Paolozzi's writings at this time and some types of Fluxus literature, which he probably encountered in West Coast literary magazines on visits to the United States. Included in *Writings* is the opening of a seventeen page novella about Hollywood and Los Angles which parodies Raymond Chandler and Dashiell Harnmett. In the late 1960s Paolozzi stepped up his writing to include a fantasy autobiography, a novel BASH (also the title of a 1971 screenprint) and several poem sequences; as well as a project with the title *New Arcadia*, probably intended as an update of Walter Benjamin, which was planned with Christopher Finch but never realized. Some material was published in the 66 page book *Abba Zaba* (1970), designed and edited with students at Watford School of Art; and occasional pieces based on material collected in America and Japan also appeared in the quarterly *Ambit* in the late 1960s and early 1970s.

This type of writing all but came to an end in the early 1970s. In the autumn of 1971 Paolozzi was given an exhibition at the Tate Gallery, but rather than the conventional retrospective which was expected, Paolozzi used the occasion to mount a critique of pop art and late modernist theory. The exhibition satirised minimalism and American post-painterly abstract painting by equating its commodification with war. On the front cover of the catalogue was an American soldiers boot, and on the back cover a pile of gold ingots each stamped '100% F* Art', which was reproduced as sculpture in the exhibition, together with a series of giant aluminium bombs, with the words of a nursery rhyme stamped on their sides; another bomb was painted yellow and had a knot tied in its tail fin. A centre piece of the exhibition was a reconstruction of a builder's skip, with the words WASTE CLOUD ATOMIC LABORATORY stencilled on its side, which contained rejected aluminium castings from the previous decade of sculpture. A twice-life sized cast of J.F. Kennedy, a 'wasted hero,' metaphorically cast off, was later added to the ensemble, which was mounted on a wooden platform to resemble Kabuki theatre. In the 1970s Paolozzi developed a form of abstract relief sculpture in sharp contrast with the brilliantly coloured figurative prints of the late 1960s which were associated with pop art. He later told me how much he regretted making art which resembled pop; perhaps unconsciously associating it with his unpublished writings which also date from the late 1960s.

Instead, in writings of the 1970s and 1980s, he turned his attention to the ecological problems of waste and pollution which continue to threaten the planet, their social and cultural reflection in certain forms of postmodern art, and citing the failure of the avant-garde to confront such issues. After his appointment as Professor of Sculpture at the Akademie der bildenden Kunste, Munich, in 1981, his writing includes essays on the relationship between the teaching of art and current notions of creativity, and the changing interpretation of the 'primitive', which was the focus of the exhibition *Lost Magic Kingdoms and Six Paper Moons from Nahuatl* (1985) based on the collections of the Museum of Mankind. In spite of some pessimism, Paolozzi's message is essentially an optimistic one for the future, and includes theoretical and practical advice for the young artist at the turn of the millennium.

In Cambridge in the summer of 1973 Paolozzi lent me a suitcase containing several hundred, possibly a thousand or two pages of writings, which I kept for nearly a year before returning it to him. Several hundred of the pages are now in the Paolozzi Archive of the Dean Gallery, Edinburgh, and are listed in Appendix 1 of the collected writings; some are still owned by the artist and others are in my own collection. In a book which includes autobiographical material, letters, statements, essays and interviews, it has not been possible to include more than a small selection of prose and poetry. When more of the writings are eventually published they will have the same distinct and unmistakeable voice of the second half of the 20th century which those of Arp and Schwitters had for the first.

ROBIN SPENCER lectures in Art History at the University of St Andrews, and is the editor of *Eduardo Paolozzi: Writings and Interviews*, forthcoming from Oxford University Press.

Selected writings

Eduardo Paolozzi

INTRODUCTORY NOTE: These pieces have been selected by Robin Spencer. Some of them will appear in the forthcoming Oxford University Press edition of Paolozzi's writings.

CURVE OF ERROR

A negro woman, hands folded across rocks with eggs
Vegetable films in the Drifters class
An anarchist, the centre circle of little gleams
Snapshots of the great Underworld rearranged
Mangled girders twisted upward, like ten o'clock
A flour-faced kid embracing outer-most steel beams
Rigid Byzantine Madonnas, tilting forward in space
Vultures, and the thump of machines stamped
Soldered joints — or has the cognac all gone?
The blind torpedo on its mile-long track
Giants fracture if the stack should fall
Death eggs dropped on black-square Mondrian

(1961)

UNTITLED

Regularly pick up the Ipswich train —
from Colchester
                passing Manningtree.
Ahistorical town on an estuary
    with a plastic factory of fair size
    by the railway tracks.
The expansion requirements causing buildings of different
complexes through the years
connected by large tubes of hut-like railway carriages
themselves.

This all running parallel with the track and all sitting
there in the middle of wild estuary life.

View of the steaming refuse dump, smoking with crows.

This viewed from the buffet car.

With my satchel of books and drawings at this time, drawings
from the Japanese rooms at the V&A —
so Kuniyashi & the plastics factory become intertwined.

Small pieces of copper with chequered silver.

                                                              (1960s)

A BAROQUE JOURNEY THROUGH THE LIMITS
OF ONE'S OWN LIMITS TO A HORIZON

Depending on Nth degrees of chance and the corroded bastions
of change, to include also important chemical changes in the
system.
The distorted actual like bottles seen through mescaline on
 a handdipped wet in sand — a tree in the snow.
But why should PROGRESSION AFFECT THIS. A carnival engine is
place at the end of construction.
TURRETS OF GEARS RAISED IN OUTLINE AT THE CAR BREAKERS
A COMPOUND OF RADIATORS
A coupled hood like an early Chinese Archer
Little Giant Frenzy plucked and placed these crusted urban
crabs the thin steel outer shells mangled punched.
Whitewashed tunnels contain in told silence black engines
laid out like the chattels of an Egyptian King.
Eyes like stingrays here. Blurred in procession, static in
shadow.
Blue-black silhouette amalgam of designed carcasses — the search
for link.

(1960s)

WILD TRACK FOR LUDWIG THE KAKAFON
KAKKOON LAKA OON ELEKTRIK LAFS

THE FIRST OF the four labyrinths, stagy, divided as it is into long dialogue
scenes formally framed by a limited number of establishing shots, yet the
teacher steps aside of the doors, the battens being held in Position by four
glorified screw eyes, as used in most theatres for a like purpose, or stout
and strong gimlets would answer, dwarfing such objects as naturally develop
to a great size, but are likewise fond of unnaturally developing objects
which in a wild state are insignificant. Aeroplanes, Horse-races, Boat races
and the like, have a certain popular value Mechanised melody Melodious
interpretation of mechanical theme … consistently medium tempo. The
continuous melody is on strings and brass with french horn predominant,
supported by staccato wood wind and muted brass phrases. Definite
ending. The buildings leaving behind only stones and bits of rubble and he
replies 'What we are destroying is nothing but houses of cards and we are
clearing up the ground of language on which they stand.' Juxtapositions,
they would find out the connections between the two pictures for
themselves. They would guess what the pictures meant to say. They would
be the artists whose imagination observe the Laocoon group with care. To
my surprise I have found several crucial restorations that have significantly
changed the composition of the group but have not been taken into account
in its recent reconstructions. The correction of these faults might choose for
example, not the white or the black box but the box which was to the right
or left, in accordance with its experience in the previous test. This would be
wheels which were of brass and had eight spokes, give the meaning but
destroy the picture. The sense is here, however, nothing; the picture
everything. Juxtapositions had been born. The plane is nearing the target.
From the inner-phones comes the pilot's warning; 'Pilot to bombardier-on
course and flying level.' As now placed, the sun seems fixed by the coils and
base that join him and his father in a relief; hour on hour they kept up this
busy whirl, stopping for neither meat nor drink, until finally the Bedouin's
horses would drop in their tracks, and the riders would fall from their
saddles, panting and exhausted. He began to give instructions, although

there were times when he felt he had dried up. He wrote a rather dull paper for the Aristotelian society but when the meeting was held, he talked of something different. Point of the composition, which in its main lines is carried up and back, like a great wave by the twisting Movement of the central figure and the complementary forms of the flanking sons. That only is the first test of the memory series would be of value as an indication of the existence of a previously acquired habit. Even under the conditions of no shock and no stop nothing is too great, nothing too trivial to ask; the heavens must resound with the blows of his hammer, and his left hand must indeed relax its hold of his sack-mouth if all petitions are granted on that day. A dull thunder, a rolling sound, from the height surrounding Rizza … it was the sound of the guns, of the wagons, of the footsteps that pulled ever towards thin wooden rods, then wound round the rods. The length of the threads must allow the actress to cross the stage and disappear into the side wings in which the action was unified in a comparatively shallow space. All this nonsense may thrill the misinformed multitudes, but its usefulness ends right there. For the flight testing of aircraft is a careful, studied science almost totally without heroics of the Hollywood variety. Two wooden partitions which are pivoted on their main vertical axes so that they could be placed in either of the positions indicated how the deepest emotion produced by the first could prejudice the one that follows. Any want of effect in the second must be owing to its inherent want of pathos. A cord A. In the diagram a forest scene is being changed into a cottage interior the bottom of the scene that moves across the stage has a few domes of silence hammered in. The sun sank with its burning arrows. The soldiers marched, bowed and grim. The air boiled thickly and threatened to choke them. The hills on the left held their breath. A solitary cloud on the horizon. Dull clothes being blown about. The actress leaning forward as though struggling against the wind, as she walks away from the manipulator of the threads. A scene of inevitable destruction. The younger son, helpless, his legs bound, his body crumpling, lapses into unconsciousness and death, fatally wounded. The band played while members of the engineering department brought out ropes and pullies, cables and derricks, beams. The general public knows little of him. But he has a softer side. He has written a poem, its last lines run 'did you hear what the bird said?' 'I did' said Algebra 'it is made in small pieces.' That a man has been taught the ordinary use of the words 'the same' in the cases of 'the same shape,' 'the same length' give point to his argument, the Grand Master then conducted his audience to another part of the forest. Can the dancer learn a regular labyrinth path more quickly than an irregular one? Now to the left, now to the right running in circles, passing through it would eliminate the extraordinary cleavage of directions. Pictorial figures may be substituted for circles. Safeguarding the operation of these elevators free flowing scrawl work designs of a floral character. Stage effects sound of heavy beams falling, which sound may be got by a muffled big drum or a heavy piece of wood, as a post is held vertically and brought down with a thud upon the stage. The band, palm up in a gesture eloquent of horror and futility, like the forearm was bent backward and down, in the direction of various sound effects required from time to time as birds singing, a policeman's or railway guard's whistle, ducks quacking, a fog horn for a ship at sea and other semi-musical instruments, all of which suffer from no lack of systematic books. No nation in the world surpasses us in the faculty of deducing from a couple of definitions and tremble at the idea of soon seeing Medea in her unmitigated ferocity, our imagination far outstripping the slightest attempt at symmetrical arrangement; indeed, anything like uniformity or balance of parts appears to be studiously avoided in these groupings. Wind is graphically expressed, birds are perched clean cut and perforate patterns the trees waving in the summer breeze, in Autumn stripping blasts, and with barren branches weighed down with winter snows; firmly anchored to the wrist, by its constricting motion the reptile also pulls the lower arm down, lifting the elbow and severely averting butterflies, and symbols of various kinds. As a distant castle suddenly becoming ruins or disappearing altogether, and a forest taking its place, or it may be an interior scene with bare walls, when instantly three houses collapsed with all their furniture, and the fire department had to be called out to prevent any explosions size, imagination can hear him cry, if he cry imagination can neither mount a step higher, nor fall a step lower without seeing him and certain elements acquire new meaning intensely baroque in nature. The younger son's death becomes a surprise, the head of the snake, that point which leaves the observer to imagine the crisis without actually showing it, and in uniting with this not so essentially transitory as to become offensive when the first company had returned. How miserable the poor devils looked with their faces pale as ashes, with weary deep-sunk eyes, he like a plane of action common to the three figures. There is, however, no continuous connection fixing this position. But his home was in Berlin, and when he laughed he opened a tremendous mouth, the simple opening of the mouth apart from the violent and repulsive contortions it causes in the other parts of the face, is a blot on a painting. The six wise men marched on as steadily as they could, for not only was the ground shaking under their feet, their knees were shaking too. They marched right out to Algebra's front door, opened it cautiously and went in. Then they got into the elevator and pushed the very top button. The assistant who manipulates the thread held a rod in each hand, giving them a see-saw motion, raising and lowering them and now and again giving them a slight pull. The above movements and others brought about by practice will serve to unify the two figures forcefully. The son's raised arm and his slightly inclined torso nicely complement the adjacent masses of the father's figure, while the raised legs are repeated motifs, wires of the interrupted circuit, it receives a shock as a result of the closing of the key in the circuit by the experimenter by means of the handle. This allows snow to gradually escape through the slots. It, the snow storm, is a prolonged one, a second assistant supplies more snow-flakes. There are some more practical aspects which conjecture is free to play upon. One lies in powers mode of understanding the world. So far Plato's problems are continuous with the modern philosophers; but they are discontinuous too in so far as neither poetry nor religion nor science not mathematics not metaphysics is now tubing, and forming, cupping, or bending sheet. The material hardens as it is worked, but the operations are seldom severe his love for irregularity gets its full scope in the disposition of his varied devices, the more we must think we see. But no moment in the whole course of an action is so disadvantageous in this respect as that of its culmination. Sky blue; white clouds; foliage green; poppies brown with black caps. Cut ovals adding triangular caps after. Clouds, free-cutting, but a few curved lines placed far above the tops of mountains or tall growing trees; when low and rain charged, they are disposed in horizontal masses across the outline of a mountain. Mist is depicted somewhat in the manner of Zipatone eccentric using Xylophone, Tymps, Piano. Mysterioso, with tymps and tambourine. He heeled down and got into a vertical dive. He was almost four hundred yards behind the bomber when he opened fire. He saw pieces of fabric disintegrate, saw the bomber weave fantastically and then a plume of black smoke issued from the starboard engine. Tympani roll, with Cymbal in unison. Rhythmic Tymps with Tambourine background. He did not paint Medea at the moment of her actually murdering her children but just before. What he thinks and knows. How to find fictional correlatives for his beliefs. The result is so violent as to extort a scream, either soon abates or it must destroy the sufferer.

(1965)

TWO POEMS FROM ABBA ZABA

STREET WALK

The rain is crying this lovely evening
a heart is wet under the moonlight
tear drop designs
who can know my tears
and who can escape the groping coming
of the black darkness

What is living dies
wherever there is life there is growth
and whatever grows lives
things are born from what lives not
and all things are changed

I had to want
most mature people want
to attach and articulate
how does it
how do we

The pursuit of my body is identical
to the pursuit of my mind
that is where I'd like to be
I lived there
or I used to.

A PICTURE POURED THROUGH PIPES OF GLASS

This whole world of pictures
is a world of symbols
flowers, colours, plants
all are symbols,
magic emblems
expressions of a spiritual world
The strongest doors in the world
the strongest and most wonderful doors in the world
Are those that guard the treasures.

(1970)

COLLAGE OR SCENARIO FOR A
COMEDY OF CRITICAL HALLUCINATION

REVOLVING ROUND the world of *Locus Solus* and *Scribble-de-Hobble* the second phase in the search for invisible meanings is composed of new texts from old books and constructions from found materials — cut-away mountains scattered with fetish objects or lost rooms strewn with giant objects (fractured if necessary); paper on wood, paint on tin, string on card, shadow on wall; Imperial ikons like ghost memories fused to the walls of a children's theatre; liquid projections to satisfy the mind; cut-out grasshoppers eat ancient generators in the foreground and on the horizon academic figures debate; wooden and iron objects rescued from abandoned ships fill the classroom — already the flags and charts are cut up for projections or zones — or inventions.

Making collage can be a symbolic art, like life itself — a tangle unravelled. Experience denied or an iconographic interpretation divorced from the niceties of formal analysis. As in a painting by Carpaccio or Bosch improbable events can be frozen into peculiar assemblies by manipulation — time and space can be drawn together into new spatial strategy. Dream and poetry can be fused without the usual concessions to graphic limitations. Figures from a Turkish landscape trapped by cruelty may be released and find themselves perplexed and frightened in a French nursery flanked by the mechanical sphinx.

A book on Rodin mentions the way the great sculptor had 'transitions' of the portraits cast so that a spontaneous stage could be held in reserve for future development. One photograph shows the large collection of legs, feet and heads made by Rodin to enable him to fabricate figures outside the limits of preconception. Plastic metaphors generated by the inner cinema of mind-a cameraless photography of the inner soul. The Rathaus in Zurich dwarfed by a frog represents not only poetic ambiguity but also a personal hypothesis.

Divine ambiguity is possible with collage — flesh marred by object or object masquerading as flesh. There is nothing astonishing in that — witness the great portaits of Arcimboldo. We have also learned to define collage as a process where dreams can be rejected and the victims exposed to ridicule. The word 'collage' is inadequate as a description because the concept should include damage, erase, destroy, deface and transform — all parts of a metaphor for the creative act itself. Preconscious elaboration must have a relationship to chance therefore the permutations of one hundred and one figures on forty landscapes and interiors represent a process of endless destruction until finalization.

(1977-9)

THE BATTLE OF THE LAPITHS AND CENTAURS

IN NO OTHER painting [has] the theme of' 'the Battle between the Centaur and the Lapiths' been more brilliantly conceived than [in] the panel by Piero di Cosimo. Artificial constructions like the centaurs and cyclops are developed in ways that seem unconsciously to emphasize the interlocking virtues and vices of nature and culture. Out of this world of aggressiveness, danger, violence, the painter weaves this tapestry into a frozen tableau of pagan horror-impulses are impulses to actions - this world is a world in which we act. Thinking and naturalism are dissolved, synthetic pragmatism is swept aside as this prima/itive world takes command. Exaggerated motion may destroy the action. Connected movements are represented as a series of pictures unconnected with each other. Kinesthetic sensations occur involuntarily - the primitive world does not only react to wishes but it also reacts to actual movements or tendencies to movement. It is also in this respect a plastic world.

It is a world full of motion and change in which the wish and action has a creative influence. But one may ask whether these phenomena of imagination are really perceptions of the pagan world. It could be a world of disintegration: and what one observes only the fragments after the destruction of configurations - as in hallucinations the object is transformed into variations under the guidance of the emotional needs of the painter. When such a transposition takes place the transposed part becomes condensed with the other parts of the experience — this primitive world of perception becomes more plastic and changeable. Transpositions in space take place — the pictures are cut into parts — movements are transformed from the moved to the unmoved; this movement has very often an unnatural character whether the figure is dressed or not.

This superb exercise in visual imagination, scintillation and fragmenta-tion of shape & curved lines, simple geometrical figures, roses, animals, other human beings in perpetual motion overlap with multiplications. Whether reality is or can be considered in a metaphysical or an epistemological light this could become a pseudo-thesis — the consequence of this, the theoretical overvaluation of aesthetics. The vertical direction of the outer world may be experienced as oblique. The big animals have a heavy mass and walk slowly. There are only four or five. The little animals are tiny — sometimes an ambiguous touch of paint. The motions fit to the mass of the objects. The motion also expresses itself in the change of faces — space, mass, people, object appear in an original psychophysiological union. It is myths above all that seem to defy rational analysis and to give rise to the idea that their makers were rambling around in a kind of mystical fog — yet closer observation, and the whole tendency of the anthropologists, treating tribal peoples with increasing respect, has shown that most of the apparently [random?] connections in primitive myths are not really so. Rather the logical systems involved are different from those standardised in western culture — we can consider the myth of the monster in the heart of the labyrinth as an extension of our own psyche. One of Jung's strongest intuitions is that men depend on ancient and traditional forms of expression, tribal and religious as well as myths, no less now than before, consigning them to the sphere of historical curiosities. This has merely increased the neurotic malady of modern man.

(1978)

DREAM - MUNICH - WEDNESDAY 16 MARCH 1989

I was climbing at nightfall with other, unknown, people through a wood to the top of a hill. As we approached the top, the hill flattened and we could see that, although it was dark, there was a tinge of red in the sky. We became more and more quiet, trying not to tread on sticks or dried leaves, as we neared the top. Finally, we lay down on our stomachs and inched our way to the edge of what turned out not to be a hill. but a precipice.

When I looked over I saw one of the most beautiful scenes I've ever dreamt. There was an almost black, glossy lake stretching below to right and left for as far as we could see. On the opposite shore were trees spaced reasonably apart and black in the dusk; they were in bud, rather than in leaf. Through them shone the last rays of sunset. It was almost like a silhouette in black and red.

As I watched, enthralled, the scene came alive. Flickers of red and silver tinged lights broke the surface here and there. At first I thought they were fireflies, but they were the wrong colour. Then I realised they were fish leaping at insects in the gathering night. The more I looked, the more I saw.

Deer darted among the tres periodically. Birds flew through the wood and landed on the branches of the trees. And finally, just under the surface of the water, we could see shapes ducking and diving. They were otters or seals - we couldn't decide which by then because the light was so bad. Then, suddenly, I heard voices from directly below me. They were whispering men's voices and I feared that the men would somehow disrupt the harmony. I tried very stealthily to see what they were up to. I strained my ear, pressing my shoulders to the precipice so as not to fall over. I became more and more frightened.

Then the non-dream telephone rang.

Background

I was in Munich for a spring holiday, part of which involved taking German lessons with, of all people, […] a beautiful woman slightly younger than me named 'X', who is the only foreign national teaching at the Goethe Institut. At my last lesson, she finished off by reading me two poems, one by Schiller and the other, 'Mondnacht' by von Eichendorf, which is reproduced below:

Es war, als hatt der Himmel	Die Luft ging durch die Felder,
Die Erde still geküsst	Die Ähren wogten sacht.
Dass sie im Blütenschimmer	Es rauschten leis die Wälder,
Von ihm, nun träumen müsst.	So sternklar war die Nacht.

Und meine Seele spannte
Weit ihre Flügel aus,
Flog durch die stillen Lande,
Als flöge sie nach Haus.

MOONLIT NIGHT

It was as though the sky had quietly kissed the Earth so that she in the glory of blossom now had to dream of him.

The breeze went across the fields, the ears of corn waved gently, the woods rustled softly, the night was so starry-clear.

And my soul stretched its wings wide and flew through the tranquil counties as though it was flying home.

(trans. Leonard Foster, *The Penguin Book of German Verse*)

'X's eyes got very misty while she was reading and translating the poem into rather rough English for me. We spoke of what an expressive word 'schimmer' was. While reading, she often stroked her hand tenderly across mine to demonstrate the words 'quietly', 'gently', 'softly'. And at the end of her reading, the tears came and she said in a choked voice, 'Oh, I am so homesick for —'

Then she composed herself bravely and went on to read the other poem by Schiller. This, too, was about longing. She had no need to translate the last two lines for me. I understood and then it was my turn to burst into tears. (Oddly enough, I can't remember anything about this poem, although I am sure I would recognise it were I to see it again.) We both looked at one another for some time without speaking and then her nice, 13-year-old son [...] came to say that it was time for me to catch my bus back to Munich.

The Paolozzi Collection at the Dean Gallery and Gallery of Modern Art

Fiona Pearson

IN 1995 THERE were two generous gifts to the Scottish National Gallery of Modern Art. First was the gift from Sir Eduardo Paolozzi of his studio contents. Second was the bequest from Gabrielle Keiller of an outstanding collection of Surrealist art together with a superb group of early Paolozzi works. These two gifts have been housed in the Dean Gallery, opposite the Scottish National Gallery of Modern Art in Belford Road, Edinburgh. In common with the Krazy Kat Arkive at the Victoria and Albert Museum's Archive in Blythe Road, Olympia, London, the Dean Gallery has become a centre for the study of the work of Paolozzi. Whereas the V&A holds mainly works on paper, tearsheets, books, magazines, toys and film memorabilia, the Paolozzi Collection in Edinburgh has 3,000 sculptures, 2,000 works on paper, 2,000 photographs, 8,000 slides, 3,000 books, 52 boxes of tearsheets and scrap material, 6 boxes of manuscripts, 100 moulds and the Spellbound exhibition installation.

The sculptures and books have been catalogued and put onto computer. Students who wish to refer to these catalogues or to the remaining uncatalogued material should contact Fiona Pearson at the Scottish National Gallery of Modern Art (telephone 0131 624 6306 direct or 6324 secretary.) Paolozzi artist's books and the Keiller Surrealist archive collection can be seen by appointment with Ann Simpson at the Dean Gallery (telephone 0131 624 6252 direct or 6324 secretary.)

The Dean Gallery has Paolozzi material on display at all times. There is the Paolozzi studio reconstruction and the adjacent Paolozzi Gallery. At present the Paolozzi Gallery has the third in a series of exhibitions exploring aspects of the artist's work. The current display of works from 1980 to 2000 features an installation of heads, figure sculpture, public project models and prints. Outside the Paolozzi Gallery are two door cases full of highlights from the Spellbound exhibition on art and cinema. On the opposite side of the corridor is the Café Newton which has a resin cast of the big sculpture Master of the Universe, photographs of the artist and door cases full of recent plaster casts. In the Great Hall there is the 27 foot high figure of Vulcan, a cubist figure exploring the theme of man and machine and the Cleish ceiling panels.

The studio reconstruction at the Dean Gallery is a facsimile of three different working areas used by Paolozzi at his London base. The room was designed by Nick Gorse, who was Paolozzi's assistant for seven years. The two desk areas flanking the entrance are dominated by work on paper cutting, information gathering, tearsheets, scrapbook folders of cut out items from magazines, books and catalogues, newspapers, glue and scissors. This is the sort of activity that takes place in the studio in which Paolozzi lives. The bed platform represents the spartan living conditions in that main studio.

In the centre of the studio at the Dean Gallery is a large table used for many years by the artist in his back studio, which is dedicated to the making of sculpture. The table has many work stations showing work in progress on heads, figures and public projects. In the foreground are raw materials such as an old piano keyboard. The walls around the studio are lined with shelves from floor to ceiling and are crammed with plaster casts, waxes, toys, model kits and rummage boxes of component parts. The layered mass of material in Paolozzi's back studio and garage represents roughly two decades of work. The human figure, animals, vehicles, geometric shapes, machinery, engines, reliefs drawn from paintings and film stills, architectural details, classical and renaissance subject matter are mixed together with the brightly coloured boxes of Star Wars kits, glove puppets, and motorbike engine models. Suitcases everywhere speak of the transport of materials, models and tools between London and Germany over several decades as Paolozzi fulfilled teaching commitments at home and abroad. Plasticised holdalls strewn across the floor are full of materials and works in transit between studio and foundry.

On another site there is archive material in the shape of original plasters and models for public projects, tearsheets, moulds and the Spellbound exhibition installation. The work of cataloguing the material in all three buildings will be completed by 2004 when a full Paolozzi catalogue will be published. In order to celebrate this event we are planning a major Paolozzi exhibition for 2004 to take up the top floor of the Dean Gallery.

In the immediate future we are planning a Paolozzi in context conference on Saturday 2 December 2000 in the Gymnasium of the Scottish National Gallery of Modern Art. Speakers will include Robin Spencer (editor of a new book of Paolozzi writings and interviews, compiler of the catalogue raisonné of Paolozzi sculpture), Philip Dodd (curator of Spellbound exhibition, Director of ICA and biographer), Malcolm McLeod (co-curator of Lost Magic Kingdoms exhibition) , Malcolm Heyes (Museum of Childhood) and Patrick Elliott (Scottish National Gallery of Modern Art). In order to be sent details, please contact Joel Edwards, Education Curator, Dean Gallery (telephone 0131 624 6255 or 6200 switchboard).

A fully illustrated publication on the life and work of Paolozzi is available from the Dean Gallery Shop price £12.95. There is also a wide range of postcards, slides and Paolozzi-designed merchandise.

BIBLIOGRAPHICS

The most comprehensive Paolozzi research was published in 'Eduardo Paolozzi', a German book by Winfried Konnertz published in 1984 by DuMont, Cologne (long out of print). The early period is covered by Dianne Kirkpatrick's 1970 Studio Vista 'Eduardo Paolozzi', and the most recent specialized English publication is Judith Collins and Richard Riley British Council catalogue, 'Eduardo Paolozzi: Artificial Horizons and Eccentric Ladders: Works on Paper 1946-1995'. The forthcoming publication of Robert Spencer, 'Eduardo Paolozzi: Writings and Interviews', OUP 2000, will include an exhaustive chronology and extended footnotes. It will be the most substantial piece of Paolozzi literature since Spencer's 1984 'Eduardo Paolozzi: Recurring Themes' catalogue. (There is a large collection of Paolozzi literature in the Paolozzi Collection.)

POST SCRIPT

Recent Paolozzi events have included the unveiling of a large figure of Vulcan in Newcastle-upon Tyne; an exhibition at the University of Northumbria; a large installation in the forecourt of the Royal Academy in London; an exhibition at his dealers, Flowers East in London and a group show of prints at Edinburgh Printmakers Workshop. Other current projects include a large seated figure for the University of Birmingham; an Oscar Wilde Memorial for Chelsea; doors for the West Front of St. Giles Cathedral, Edinburgh; stained glass windows for St Mary's Episcopal Cathedral, Edinburgh and a set of prints dedicated to the life and work of Alan Turing.

FIONA PEARSON works at the Scottish National Gallery of Modern Art and is the author of *Paolozzi* (SNGMA, 1999)

Four Haiku

Alan Spence

this spring evening
blue estuary light
vast empty sky

the tiny cloud of
the cat's breath
on the windowpane

I know I will die
but still…
the full round moon

crossing the bridge —
the other side
is lost in mist

ALAN SPENCE's recently published work includes the paperback edition of *Way to Go* (Phoenix) and the introduction to the Canongate Classics edition of *The Changeling* by Robin Jenkins. These haiku are taken from his forthcoming collection *Seasons of the Heart*, published by Canongate. He is currently writer in residence at the University of Aberdeen.

Six poems

Brian Johnstone

BODY LANGUAGE

These gestures carry ordinary words,
cross-pollinating in the palm,
                              a semblance
of the self as watermarks
observed in paper
                    held up to the light.

Rehearse this choreography of instinct,
this placing
              of response to threat in moves
which tax the muscles less than merely
                    stepping off the kerb.

In the raising of an eyebrow,
                              the outward
spreading of a hand, is something like desire,
some furtive point
                    not quite
within our grasp:
                    a template cut for marquetry,
                    the hidden contours of a map.

THE ARCHAEOLOGY OF MESO-AMERICA
(The Zoque excavations, Rio La Venta, Mexico)

This was a bundle of bones long before
it was a boy. Wrapped in the shawl
of a womb, contained, perhaps

at such a moment marked for something more
that brought him here. We feed on this:

the past, that room beyond the gallery
hollowed from the rock. And there,
in galaxies of dust, deliver these:

a leather bracelet, a brooch of pumpkin rind,
a bag that held his torn asunder limbs.

We say: we must retreat from our beliefs,
understand his blood, as it soaked into the bark
burned for life, for light within

the hollow of his skull, sliced through,
we see, to taste the substance of his thought.

THE TRAIN NOW WAITING

'With the old railwaymen ... it was part of your life ... railways went
through the back of your spine like Blackpool went through rock.'

'The Ballad of John Axon' — Ewan MacColl,
Peggy Seeger & Charles Parker

There you go once more, placing
your foot on the plate, pulling
at levers. This fire is firing up your days.

Watch the clock. Pitch its numbers round
inside your head. Believe it, passing
over those beams, rubbing gabardine to a fine gloss

where there is nothing now, space
filled with hogweed, dead nettle, the detritus
of late shoppers, drinkers on the lam.

Nothing new. And you unlikely to stop,
stationary in your boots, a waxy sheen. Your place
on the step: what was it? A dream.

OUTSIDER
for Angus McPhee

These were his ordinary shoes,
this his ordinary vest, this shirt
he could have worn this rough
and fibrous on his skin; each
woven blade, each seed head, stalk,
each thread of root replacing loss
with need. You realise it was his life.
No measure could exist to take
that sleight of hand from fingers
that had known it, such as these.
And these his ropes twined:
seasons, days and hours sown in
like bits of leaf or bark, their spirits
stitched about him, worn until
he laid them on the ground.
This ordinary creel, that harness
hanging by the wall, each one
an offering, an ordinary thing
from hands that plead, insist
they have none else to give.

And give this ordinary gift.

Note: From the work of outsider artist Angus McPhee, most of whose life
was spent in psychiatric hospital, where he created a series of woven gar-
ments and artifacts now preserved in the archive of The Scottish Collection
of Art Extraordinary. First published in *Angus McPhee, Weaver of Grass* by
Joyce Laing

AN ATTEMPT AT CONTAINMENT
for Mateusz Fahrenholz

These things are placed in boxes:
intelligence, precision, belief;
a containing of space.

Without, the factual air, the lie
of the surface, history
in a patina of time.

Within, worlds spin through gestures,
the material eyes of faces
turned this way, that.

The machine is here, burnished
with purpose, an energy latent
in form and thought.

Believe it, it is real, tensioned shut.
Prize that part of it, mercury
in your hand's palm.

These things are placed in boxes:
that which is and is not.
Work with it.

It is the receptacle you require.

REASON

Perhaps it will occur to you
on examining a slide, on polishing
the auriole of a lens. Perhaps
you will sense it in the low hum
of the plant, or even in the creaking
of light incessant rain.
                        You might
define it thus.
                  An urge to flinch,
to flick the bed clothes back up
to the chin, to curl into a ball
and have no more to say.
                        There is
no more to say.
                  What you will do
is step back, glance across the room
and place your hands before you
on the bench. They tremble. Light
seeps through the window with some
vague intent. You turn to polishing
the lens, your sightless eye.

BRIAN JOHNSTONE is a poet, writer and photographer, published widely in Scotland, as well as in Greece and Poland. His collection *The Lizard Silence* was published by Scottish Cultural Press in 1996 and his next publication is due from Akros, in August 2000. He was awarded a Scottish Arts Council Writer's Bursary in 1998 and is currently Chairman of *StAnza* Poetry Festival. He is employed as creative writing tutor for both the Open College of the Arts and St Andrews University Centre for Continuing Education.

Brian and Ringo

Hannah McGill

Saturday night he tried to keep his key a secret in the lock, but Stella's ears, though tiny, were sharp, and she threw open the bedroom door to welcome him. The glare of the hallway's naked bulb threw her feline face into sharp relief against her black curls; she wore only a little skirt and a white bra. There was glitter streaked across her cheekbones and music blared out of the room. Connor heard David, behind her, say something incoherent and then laugh. Connor lived amongst a clutter of records and amplifiers and old magazines with David and Sean. Stella lived somewhere else, but she was always there, especially at night.

'Con-nor,' said Stella, sleepily, eyes very wide and thin arm extended. 'Connor! Join us — c'mon — c'mon — c'mon.'

David shouted: 'Yeah, Con, whatcha doin', man? Come in, we're — playing music, and —'

'We're DANCING,' Stella said, drawing a handful of hair over her face. 'We're dancing and —' she laughed and looked at the ceiling — 'hey, hey, Con, have you got anything to eat?'

'Cigarettes, man,' David drawled, still out of sight. Connor moved towards Stella, taking his fags from his pocket. She bent down and took them in her mouth. He followed her into the little room as she dropped to her knees and delivered them to David, who was reclining shirtless on his bed, a mattress on the floor. He too was touched with glitter, and the pair of them twinkled in the pinkish light from a dilapidated lava lamp as they lit cigarettes, giggling. Connor smiled a little, like a parent watching his child play with a puppy. Stella lay back and cast wide her arms, her ribcage rising as pronounced as the keys on a xylophone. Looking at the lava lamp beside her, she said, 'This has gone all... furry and weird inside. It's sort of gross. It was so HOT today. We had to stay in bed. Con, you should lie down with us.'

'There isn't room,' he told her quietly.

'We can MAKE room,' she said. He moved closer to the bed and crouched beside them. David's smile spread out and Stella's sharp hands reached over him to touch Connor's face. She kissed him dryly, her hair in David's face; he felt heat radiate from her skin. She scrambled to her feet again then, and clumsily changed the record, while David lazily smiled and asked Connor, 'Where were you, man?'

'Out with Rick and Sean and Carl.'

David looked blankly, blinked twice.

'Carl, man, how's Carl?'

'OK. OK. He's DJing at the Duke tonight.'

'That'll be great...'

The record skipped and skidded because Stella was jumping up and down next to it, shaking her head and crying, 'Connor, dance with me, Connor.' Awkwardly he got to his feet and moved to her, stumbling on discarded shoes; she held him very close and sang loud in his ear. Her breasts were small and hard like those of a much younger girl; her pelvis dug into him.

'Con dances so great, Davy... dance with Con. You two should DANCE.'

Her head was lolling to one side, her balance gone. She waded over to David, pulled him to his feet and slumped on the mattress. 'Davy, give Con a kiss because he brought us... fuckin'... cigarettes. Cigarettes.'

David stood unsteadily. His taut stomach bore a neat line of hair; his body was muscular, rounded, closely packed. He lurched at Connor lovingly and almost knocked him down; their teeth clashed in a wet, laughing kiss that sent a shock of heat through Connor.

'Ah, fuckin' great, man, fuckin'...'

David fell heavily against Connor, arms around him, and Connor gripped him too, feeling sweat and grains of glitter on the smooth skin of his back. Just as quickly though they slid apart again; David picked up a bottle, swung away, nudged Stella with his foot. She was curled in sudden sleep, saliva at the corner of her mouth, her hands half-fists. Connor noticed suddenly the haze of smoke in the room; his tiredness overwhelmed him and he found himself back in the doorway, leaning against the frame, the wood cold and solid on his cheek. He went to bed, but they were noisy late into the night; David must have woken Stella, because she mewed like a cat till almost dawn.

Monday the weather broke. It was sudden. Connor was sitting in the beer garden with Sean, weary and sick from the heat, when thunder rolled over them and rain began to pelt on to the canopy above them. Sean leapt up and out into the downpour, whooping, colliding with people rushing back inside the pub for shelter; he spread his arms and turned his face to the rain before turning back to Connor with a frown.

'Don't fancy lugging all the equipment in this.'

Connor peered at the leaden sky.

'Summer shower. Won't last. Besides, there's not that much; it won't take long.'

Sean, water streaming down his face, nodded happily and spun, skidding on the wet grass, a complete revolution.

'Did you see the graffiti in the bogs about Stel?'

Connor shook his head, bur Sean wasn't looking at him, so he said, 'No.'

'It says, "How did that wee poof Davy King pull such a gorgeous bird?"'

Connor laughed.

'What do you reckon about that?'

'Well… she is.'

Sean returned to the table, shaking water from his hair like a dog. 'I don't go for Stel.'

'Everyone goes for Stella.'

'Don't get it, man. She's good looking, but…'

'She's skinny.'

'Ah, there's just… there's something not there. She likes you, though. Always talking about you.'

'I was dancing with her last night.'

'The glitter and the dancing again, eh? What are those two like?'

'I think they just got a whole lot of stuff off Barney.'

'What about this fucking rain, man…? Davy does remember about the gig, doesn't he?'

'Oh, yeah. However out of it he gets he always remembers.'

'Always plays all right as well.'

'Talented wee guy.'

'Imagine what he'd be like if he practised.'

'Imagine what you'd all be like if you practised.'

'You know what Rick thinks about that.'

'Spontaneity.'

'Spontaneity, man.'

They listened to the splatter of raindrops on tarpaulin above them. All other noise seemed to have ceased. The playpark opposite had been swiftly evacuated, the children stowed neatly away in the surrounding tenement flats. A couple of student-looking girls rushed by, soaked and shrieking, in summer vests and sandals. Connor watched Sean watching them, wet fabric clinging to slim thighs, calves and arms shiny with water and hair flying in strings.

'Your round,' said Sean.

'What are you drinking?'

'Cider.'

'Cider? What, are you nostalgic for your schooldays?'

'I didn't drink at school.'

'What did you do?'

Sean lit a cigarette and said, 'Acid.'

'At school?'

'The acid, the jellies, the pills, man, the fuckin'… everything.'

'I thought you were a public schoolboy?'

'Yeah. No chicks, see. Had to do something.'

Sean's smile showed his broken front tooth, a flaw that, like his other flaws, seemed to work to his advantage. He had the look of some sixties pop urchin, some little Peter Noone character; wide jaw and high up cheekbones, big crooked smile and childish skin. Later on he vanished with Carla and wasn't seen for three or four days.

The rest of the week it rained on and off, and the hot, dusty smell of summer streets first intensified and then washed away.

Friday night Connor was slumped on the floor of Sean's room, trying, blearily, to pick out a record. He had come into the room with something specific in mind but had been distracted by variety, new acquisitions. Sean didn't buy things, but he always had lots of new possessions, picked up, borrowed, stolen here and there. A commotion in the hallway marked his return,

'Don't go near that fucker, he's got fucking herpes!'

'Jesus, don't touch anything, you dirty cunt.'

'I do not have herpes. I have cold sores.'

'It's August!'

'What's Carla say about it?'

'Carla?'

'He's not seeing her any more.'

'She was all right.'

'That's putting it mildly...'

'But then I met her sister.'

'Does she have cold sores too?'

Laughing, Sean came into his room.

'You wanna watch yourself,' Connor said, without allowing himself to look up. Sean took off his shirt and flung it down.

'Can I help it if they love me?'

Connor looked at him then. He was looking in the mirror, inspecting the scabs around his mouth. There was a livid mark on the side of his neck and another on his shoulder. Connor gazed, feeling muzzy-headed. He'd been drinking all day, and smoking, doing all the work too because Davy was too lazy to skin up and Rick claimed he didn't know how, although Con suspected this to be a labour-saving excuse.

'Sean, it's hard not to,' he said, and had to leave.

He got out on to the street and then didn't know what to do. It was deserted. The streets were glistening, the streetlights and shop signs reflected in wet smears, though the rain had stopped. He headed unsteadily across the road, intending to buy cigarettes in the blinding brightness of the 24-hour Spar, but by the time he'd felt out the right money in his pocket, and debated with himself whether or not he was going to be able to make himself understood, he'd gone past it. His head was pounding; he felt sick and ashamed, though the reason for this slipped in and out of focus in his head, appalled him and then evaded him. He couldn't remember, about eight blocks down the road, exactly what had precipitated his departure, but his eyes seemed wet. He ignored a voice behind him, expecting abuse. Then footsteps neared him, and he recognised David's voice, breathless. He turned.

'Con, man — I've run — fuckin' miles after you — you twat — where the fuck you going?'

David bent over, hands on his knees, to catch his breath. Con said nothing and then, 'Why did you come after me?'

'Sean said — you were weird. I wanted to make — sure — you were all right. Fuck. I haven't run like that since school.'

Con sat on a damp garden wall and David joined him. 'Give us a fag, man, I need to get my breath back. What are you doing out here, for fuck's sake? It's miserable.'

They lit fags and Con put his heavy dizzy head in his hands. David patted him loudly on the back and Con felt like a half-drowned kitten being shaken back to life. He made a strange sound. 'What the fuck's wrong, man? Are you worried about the gig or that? All those record company fuckers? Cos you know it always pulls together in the end, like.'

'I know. I know.'

'We don't need a manager, man, we need a fuckin' babysitter, eh? Did you take one of they dodgy pills Barney had?'

'No.'

'You all right like? Gonnae be sick?'

Tears had begun in earnest now, and Con thought that what had started him off was a sudden memory of a babysitter he'd once had who had slapped him when he wouldn't sleep. He was too far gone to be embarrassed, but he felt sorry for David, who was so mild, so without guile or unkindness, that he was difficult to fathom at the best of times. He spoke stumblingly and without much notion of what he was saying.

'You know what I'm like? What I… feel like I mean. I feel like… Brian fucking Epstein.'

There was a pause in which David inhaled thoughtfully.

'Nah, man. You're no like him. Cos see if you're Brian Epstein, that makes us the Beatles, which makes me fuckin' Ringo, and I'm not gonnae be Ringo for anybody, cos I'm the good looking one in this band, all right?'

Con didn't think for long enough to wonder whether David knew what he meant or not, just allowed himself to be led back to the flat and given water. He calmed down. People went to bed, went home. Sean, drunk, his prettiness all suddenly spoilt and sore, danced again, in the middle of the room.

'Con, mate, Con, mate, I can't — I can't stop spinning, mate, I can't—'
'You can.' Con placed his arms clumsily around Sean's neck and tried to stop the movement. Their faces collided hard, cheekbone against jaw. Con smelled dirty hair, sweat, cigarettes and traces of old shampoo, all brought out by rainwater.
'Can't stop, can't stop,' Sean repeated, stopping.

The vodka ran out some time, some time late. After that, not much more happened.

HANNAH McGILL was born in Shetland and grew up in Lincoln. She graduated from Glasgow University last year and now works as the television critic for *The Scotsman*. She is currently working on her first novel.

from The Prada Meinhof Gang

Drew Milne

CLUELESS, AS IF

Well honestly, I've never seen such a collection of balding sour goats as
there were in that room last night. I mean, there were cadavers wherever you
looked. Brian's the most joyless. I hope for her sake that his new girlfriend
has a sense of humour. I pity any woman who depends on him to light up
their day. What's the world coming to? It's not as if you could accuse me of
not putting out. But oh no, the bons mots fall on stony ground with all the
bounce of a dead cat thrown from a moving train. That Samuel character,
what's his name, wouldn't even look me in the eye. And there's a limit to the
pleasure a girl can extract from batting her eyelids at a tasty array of canapés.
It must be a measure of something that party food has replaced alcohol as
the principal sensual distraction. From my point of view the bold physical
gestures of fizzy wine ought to convey the promise of light chit-chat and
together with a resourceful use of stage-space a good time is had by all. Let
the dancing commence. But no, it's all about balancing envy on the end of
a gloomy sigh and tossing the word-salad with the spice of dismay. The
dead-end job and the price of housing, boo-hoo. And it can only get worse.
Short of hiring some professional comics to do sketches about middle-class
hypochondria in the hope that satire might delay the inevitable, we can look
forward to an increasingly Jacobean array of ailments and exits. Before we
know where we are we'll all be Tony's cronies in death by a thousand blunt

kitchen knives, co-starring Jerry Savalas as the hirsute but shagged-out angel of the apocalypse, with Lucinda Bonham-Cartier back from the grave to rescue her dentures. And by the way, I never understood what you saw in that posh girl pout thing. If you ask me, it's all lips and no teeth, a great soup of lazy eyelids and languid vowels. I'd rather be poisoned by good intentions and the embrace of a personal trainer than find myself stuck with a herd of her kind in the waiting room for self-service execution. If I didn't know better I'd say you were a snob beneath that veneer of plausible deniability. It's all very well adopting a policy of gentle diplomacy, but as far as I can see the only solution is to stoke things up a bit, send in the odd reminder that all's fair in love and war, let them know that this here special relationship can't be taken for granted. Either that or it's all up with fun, fur and flirting, show me the way to go home. Speaking of which, isn't it time we started a family of our own? Then we'd have nobody but ourselves to blame if the conversational wit and domestic glamour reflected an unhealthy lack of social intrigue. We could do jelly, coke and e-numbers, play musical chairs without fear of interruption, and then watch the gradual realisation of hormonal destiny wipe the smile off their angelic little faces, before the onset of full-scale surliness becomes a joy to behold.

COMING UP FROM THE STREET

There was something in the swagger with which she took on the city that made you want to press the pause button to see how she did it. It was a kind of amiable miracle. Our team had been pounding the archives in search of that extra something to incorporate in the latest campaign. Whatever it was, she had that something: spontaneity, clarity and a kind of affirmative drive that shook off centuries of typecasting and negative profiling. More importantly, it had a black power that showed no nostalgia for the tired moves of Europe, a power that could speak to the pleasures of an integrated society in search of emotional confidence. Clarity amid the thrills of exertion is one of the fundamentals of classicism. Success in today's climate demands something more, a co-efficient from the human grace of nature which can speak to the romanticism in all of us. With increasingly numb dismay we had been scanning for that gesture, that look which shouted about the now, which said here is a moment of transcendence from the sorry tale of soulless over-determination. There was no doubting the ingenuity of the up-and-coming talent. But whether it was the crude quality of the moving images currently on offer, or whether there were just too many places to pick up the old orthodoxies, there was something nauseating about the available stock of reality. After a particularly gruelling session, Mariella and I had taken a stroll into the heat of the afternoon, hoping to recharge the batteries with a hint of something darker than studio lighting. We had taken the long way round, so as to avoid the ubiquitous franchised coffee-shop, in search of what might lurk off the tracks, when Mariella nearly winded me, such was the energy with which she poked me in the ribs. That poke meant eyeball alert and no talking. It took me a few seconds to revise my preconceptions. And then I saw it, about ten metres ahead, this creature just walking like she was born to move. There were a couple of swanky shoppers between her and us. Pretty soon they went into some rough-house boutique promising enamelled badges and vegetarian shoes. And then we had an uninterrupted view. Experience had given me the capacity to see how style is put together, but I couldn't deconstruct this. Among the mass of recorded nonsense, nothing had prepared me for the sheer originality of such a combination of moves. Later I tried to work backward, so to speak, from the image that remained with me after the moment had passed. Even then there was something clumsy about the simplifications I imposed in order to make memory analytic. I wanted to devote my life to the task of repeating and prolonging that swing, that groove. Grace in motion is an especially pleasurable form of fellow feeling, but I have rarely been so confident. We had discovered a star.

THE DEMOCRATIC HOME SERVICE

Wide awake industrially and intellectually enlightened as never before, the land nevertheless smouldered with apathy. A small country exhausted by theologies of identity till it was riven by racial feuds and family rivalries had scarcely afforded itself the luxury of a public sphere. The long shadow of history was wrapped like a cloak round the affairs of the present. Some blamed the constitution. A group of reformers even called for the restoration of the monarchy to stabilise the wobbly wheels of free speech and human rights. Others among the better minds of the age sought fresh shoots in the student movement. But as so often on these occasions, the spasmodic efforts of troubled individuals proved to be utopian rather than evolutionary. In pamphlets and newspapers it was the economic situation that was most dwelt upon, but the fruits of liberalisation were slow in coming. The call was often heard for greater involvement in debates of the day and that it was the duty of every citizen to speak, as if they were perfectly acquainted with all the hidden springs of government. But like efforts to damp down consumer confidence, the calls fell on deaf ears. To judge by the reports of pollsters and focus groups, the military remained popular, though little weight should be attached to resolutions passed in meetings practically closed to free expression and external corroboration. The contagion of opinion which nevertheless spread during that long winter of discontent reached the north with all the virulence of the influenza which seemed to accompany it. An outbreak of hissing greeted a local dignitary at an important sporting occasion. Such events were traditionally thought successful as pressure valves of discontent, even providing an outlet for hooligan elements scarcely tolerable anywhere else, so the omens looked serious indeed. The authorities recognised that a long-term struggle for legitimation was beginning, but although they held all the cards they lacked the political imagination with which to finesse the situation. Years of miserly support for thought had left the civil service bereft of ideas. A cloud hung over the great halls of power and myths of origin were being cooked up in the recording studios like there was no yesterday. Suffer me, wrote one mischievous scamp, to rouse you from the lethargy that has become near universal. Ingenious lawyers set upon a long drawn-out consultation process with structural readjustment as the carrot with which to distract an already dazzled populace. But it remains to be seen whether those with major interests at stake can escape public scrutiny. They know who they are, but have traditionally relied on anonymity and are thus poorly equipped to channel potential sources of support. The press, at least, remain loyal to the status quo, but this is hardly surprising given the lax attitude to media barons shown by all parties.

LIMELIGHT

She disdained conventions and did nothing to dispel rumours surrounding her high living. Loose is good, she would protest, while looking round to check that her audience would keep things strictly off the record before venturing upon the demotic. Who wants to be a tight-arse, especially when you've got shoulder-pads for protection. Who indeed. Our family is not our fate, she would declare, it is only those we love who become the family we have made. Such grandstanding hardly endeared her, perhaps because we sensed that self-fashioning creativity would become destructive if and when the times became darker. Accepting her passion to erase the past was a bond of loyalty among her entourage. Illegitimacy attracts little stigma among those who perform for a living, even among the most fervently hypocritical tabloid readers. Her origins in what used to be called the shadowy world of the courtesan might nevertheless arouse a flurry of twitches in the south coast towns where she plied her trade so effectively. Association with the faded grandeur of aristocratic prostitution might also have lent her a protective aura against the smothering love of suburbia. Discarded admirers have suggested that her violent *crises de nerfs* were themselves a way of acting out this disdain for the ordinary and their civilities. And perhaps she did over-reach our patience in her need to live up to the adjective 'stormy'. Some outbursts were undoubtedly part of a political strategy to handbag doubters into submission. It became known in later years that her struggles with unfortunate hairstyles had been a calculated ploy to prepare audiences for her emergence in new and more serious roles. The feminists seemed to admire her ability to put her self together amid the corpsing that afflicted her peers. And for interviews she affected what the voice coaches called estuary enunciation so as to suggest the vaguest allure of class struggle beneath polished accomplishment. She was determined that hostility to the fruity accent she had acquired to get on in the profession would not now, by some cruel postmodern twist, stand between her and power. We would laugh together with peculiar intensity listening to the regal vowels in those awful films from the forties. Oh darling, I only want to make you heppy, she would shout from the behind the fridge door while mixing a drink too far, with the 'e' pronounced to rhyme with hep as in hepcats, if that doesn't sound too previous. Bohemia is a moveable feast. She even made one of her underlings suggest to the royal family's advisors that their vowel movements were too plummy for the voters of middle England. Unlike those with a more vested interest in the masquerade of continuous power, she was a dog happy to learn new tricks.

IF I COULD HAVE THE FIRST SLIDE PLEASE

Our journey began many years ago with my first steps beyond the homestead. I had no idea, then, how many barren and inhospitable landscapes I would traverse in search of women who for centuries have personalised their domestic environment and made it a unique tribute to the resilience of our species. Much has been written concerning vernacular architecture and the patriarchal habitus of decorative colour, but few articles record the contribution women themselves have made. Emigration to the cities has disrupted the ancient rhythms and many traditions are now vanishing. In remote towns and villages the younger generation has begun to reject the very idea of tradition. I found extraordinary sectarian graffiti in the north, though political upheaval and the harsh climate prevented me from returning. Despite such privations, women have always found ways to bring a dash of something to the world's vile surface. I was so moved by the hard lives that women lead, especially those eking out life in isolation, that I could not leave their tasks and burdens unacknowledged. Very often, when I arrived in a street — alone and heavy with camera equipment — they would avoid eye contact, much less conversation. The men seemed obsessed by the idea that images of their women would be sold on, though I assured them that my research was honourable. Although I am an accomplished tea drinker, I had never encountered the elaborate, drawn-out ceremonies so fundamental in many homes. I had to rely on humour and body language to win the women's trust, and as I spent time with them, scarves would slip to reveal tattoos and then the inner sanctum of graffiti. On my last trip I was joined by my colleague Catherine, who was as much at ease having her hands hennaed or dipped in mushy peas as she was bouncing over rough terrain or poignantly attempting to carry a woman from a burning building. During our travels we encountered difficulties involving drugs and arms, though we were ably supported by local staff whose identity, alas, must remain a secret. One official, a handsome gentleman in his forties, was one of the kindest, gentlest and most obliging. He soon understood that by accompanying us he would have an opportunity to enrich himself spiritually and professionally. He seemed elated to have found a part of his forgotten heritage no more than thirty miles from his office, but which he would never have found alone, satisfied as he was with the status he had attained. With mixed feelings I must concede that our efforts were rarely so rewarding. There was generally only one way to reconcile our needs with those we visited, and that was to buy all of their merchandise. This was either beyond our means or likely to destroy the very lifestyles we sought to record. Behind every photograph, then, is an adventure, and the hope that beyond adventure lies solidarity.

MOVERS AND SHAKERS

Esme is well known around the circuit as a woman who refined her tastes with the precision of a master craftsman. She certainly served a long apprenticeship in the business before going on to take her current position at the helm. A decade later her flare and panache are still evident, combining the classical and the contemporary with effortless aplomb, never afraid to shock the system with innovative new ideas on policy and presentation. Although trained as an academic, she swiftly moved into more profitable pursuits, overcoming the great sloth of bookishness that has bedevilled so many of her contemporaries. In a culture which has fetishised texts, she has a remarkable capacity for visual thinking, for making those subtle connections which make us see afresh what has languished unnoticed before our slumbering gaze. She rather candidly admits that she always knew her interest would become a profession, but her private sphere, from which she co-ordinates her many commissions, remains pleasingly uncluttered. It's almost as if this guru of mess could turn the negativity of space into the ultimate chaos of interiority just by looking at it. When I put this to her, she demurred, saying that when you are constantly cultivating the image you need a blank canvas onto which to project your fantasies. She attributes her success to luck and unfailing energy. One can't help but feel that having the courage to take her opportunities at the right time also required a precocious depth of self-knowledge. One way or another she has never looked back. She couldn't do it without an exceptional support staff, and the team she has put together have become the people to know. With that frankness which has brought a smile even to her detractors she also remains unashamedly up-beat about the power of art to transform our lives. It can give you a lot of oomph for your pennies, she chuckles. Especially in the hands of a woman who knows a bargain when she sees one. She recently became a mother, and her baby daughter is already bringing out a whole new conceptual approach which we can expect to see more of in the future. The shape of things to come is a playground, apparently, in which childish dreams come to life in the wonder that is style and good living. Elegance with an amusing twist is set to be replaced by a brash, feel-good plasticity which will leave the forces of conservatism gasping for breath. Whatever else you might think about her designs on our life, you can be sure they won't be dull.

THE DEVIL IN THE DETAIL

Congratulations! You've done it. You've had a baby. I know it seems like yesterday we were all in short trousers, watching the telly and believing that things could only get better. Now we have children of our own, only this time we're watching *Teletubbies* and still believing that things can only get, well, easier. Nothing, quite simply nothing, can prepare you for the shock and the sheer exhilaration of a tiny little bundle of needs. And your own mixed bag of physicalities and bubbling fears will have to be put on hold while you sort out that burgeoning sprawl of baby debris. Keep your feet on the ground. I know that being told to follow your natural instincts feels like being given another little puddle of baby sick on your already heavy shoulder. We've all been there or there'd be no species to speak of. Put simply, there are no easy ways out, no comforting clichés you won't tire of, and no way that you too can burst your lungs with frustration. You feel like a refugee in your own living room, but anxiety isn't going to help anyone. Still, we can't help being concerned about the future all the same. They'll go off and make their own mistakes, and that's the point. The ancient wisdoms won't wash. Live in the light of your own potential for growth, that's the art of flexibility, and you don't need an infant development system designed to boost their inborn talents just to teach them that. The secret is in the little things, learning to tolerate the ups and downs, abandoning the old ideas about obedience and submission. Nowadays our aim should be to promote kids who are strong-willed but co-operative, and that just takes time and patience, the patience that gets things wrong without biting off heads. There's no point imagining they're from heaven. Before you know where you are, that tempestuous toddler with an eye for sharp objects will balloon into a brooding teenager who'd rather stew in her own sulk than say thank you. But we need to treasure the changes before they're gone in a flash. Many of our oldest friends say that the hardest thing is learning how not to compete, how not to feel like you're acting dumb. Speaking from experience, I'm in favour of tantrums because they help children gauge what appropriate behaviour is all about. Let them take an inch and they'll have you on the floor, but sometimes you have to tear up the rule book and make things up as you go along. Of course, there's a time and a place for all that guff about the real you, but even confirmed sceptics like ourselves had to come to terms with the fact that we'd have become needy-weedy parents if we hadn't been prepared to seek advice from professionals. So the next time the cute little thing throws a wobbly in the supermarket, smile serenely and imagine that there's a lack in all of us, even the loudest little noise box, it's just a question of finding the right buttons. It's easy when you know how.

SEEN BUT NOT HEARD

Until eight-year old Jim arrived at the Municipal Adventure Playground for the summer play scheme, he hadn't quite cottoned on to what the family were doing to him, or where he was headed. But as soon as he caught sight of the top of the climbing frame, his dear little heart skipped a beat and he bounded from the car like a big fluffy Labrador out of the back of a Volvo estate. He shouted out his finest bloodcurdling war cry, words to the effect of, Wowee bonzer, home again! And for many youngsters, some of them with their own particular special needs, the playground is just that — a home from home. The Playground's only drawback is the demand placed by others on this idyllic setting. It's not just the kids that can't get enough of its warm embrace and sunny groves. But what the place affords for the lucky few is more than money can buy, the freedom to play like nowhere else, to be that little person inside rather than a marked child in a world of surveillance cameras and security guards. Just as a proud mum is explaining this to my photographer and I, a child who looks to be about seven and a half streaks by starkers with muddy locks flapping in the summer sun. Looking at her sunny face you have to say that she's having the time of her life. Amid the trees there are sand pits, paddling pools, specially modified wheely bins, huge wooden thrones and various imaginary states that change daily according to the magical whims of make-believe. Indoors, there is a softly padded play area, where children can quite literally bounce off the walls, and enough distractions to last a month of I'm-bored-mummy Mondays. There's no secret about the success of all this. The child comes first. As the play-leader explains, When it comes to having a good time, it's the kids who are the real experts. As play-workers, our role is to take our cue from them. The fruits of this approach suggest a radical rethink in the way we organise the world of leisure. The ameliorative effects on young ones with mild autism are most encouraging. But this takes expensive one-to-one attention from qualified adults, and I'm here to publicise the importance of this in the face of council cut-backs. Mostly the playground survives on voluntary contributions from local parents, though there is a rigorous system of vetting and scholarships to ensure that parents don't get preferential treatment on the basis of income alone. A diverse range of backgrounds is as important to those who run the scheme as financial security, and in the field of special needs it is almost always the poor who come last. Jim, for example, is a bright child from a troubled background who has been on the Special Needs Register for years. Since coming to the Playground his dyspraxic tendencies have stabilised and although still suffering from hyperactive spells, his anti-social behaviour has been improved by the sort of loving telling-off that the scheme provides. The inevitable conflicts are now resolved quietly and with good humour.

PURE FICTION: A CRITIQUE

It was Sunday. A glass too many of the violently chilled Chardonnay and the guards began to drop. I forget who it was that slipped first, but before long all sorts of risqué revelations were competing for air-play. It was all I could do to keep from wetting myself. With the prospect of boozy shopping among the great and the good it felt like a grand way to relax. We were all in the same boat. The wine somehow encouraged us to believe that client confidentiality was safe in our hands. Besides, like true professionals, we changed the names. I shudder to think what the protagonists of our gabfest would think if they knew. Having said which, it's not as if you needed a Phd in criminology to figure out roughly who was involved in the developing roman-fleuve of our little Gathering. As if to acknowledge as much, the most obvious symptom of transferable guilt was Elspeth's acid drop to the effect that the so-called scientific proceedings were hardly a good advert for the stringency of the institute's self-criticism. If that lot didn't need group therapy, you could call her the bionic woman. Jean suggested that we could leave auto-critique to the Maoists, but Arthur tried to top that with some rambling anecdote about a colleague he'd been co-teaching with at the university. To cut a long story short, Arthur had convinced his colleague that the effect of Thatcherism on the academic community was analogous to the cultural revolution. For return to rice fields read the imposed jargon of academic audit and transferable skills: hey presto, dunce hats all round. Jean restored morale by suggesting that the proceedings now read more like the shadow-boxing of the Gang of Four before the creation of the SDP. It hardly amounted to a conspiracy to shake the foundations of Western metaphysics, though an impressive degree of symbolic violence had been sublimated. The unrepresented violence of the mother and daughter relationship was on all our minds after a fine seminar paper we'd been discussing. It was at this point that Ricardo butted in with the story of a woman he'd been treating for years. It seemed that her mother was a feminist, determined to reveal the full gory story of teenage angst and the revisionary implications for women's relation to power. Her daughter was sure that all her friends would discover the most lurid details. Her mother nevertheless refused to fictionalise her identity to protect her from recognition. She'd changed her name, become estranged from identity as such, and was knee-deep in a full-scale Electra complex. We agreed that fiction was always the better part of discretion, and that it was the mother that needed treatment. Perhaps the thought of betrayal made us sheepish as regards the evident violence of the quasi-fictional indiscretions we'd been revelling in. We were consoled by the thought that the insistence on the whole truth belonged in the trash can, along with the Protestant work ethic.

DREW MILNE was born in Edinburgh in 1964. Previous publications in *Edinburgh Review* include 'NOSTALGIA' (no.90) and 'Aggropolis' (no.95). He co-edited *Marxist Literary Theory: A Reader* with Terry Eagleton (Blackwell: 1996). Recent books of poetry include *Songbook* (Akros: 1996), *Bench Marks* (Alfred David Editions: 1998), *Pianola* (Rem Press: 2000) and *The Gates of Gaza* (Equipage: 2000).
Homepage: http://drewmilne.tripod.com

Three Poems

Howard Wright

FRIDAY NIGHT HOTEL

Its ferro-concrete exterior, the retro-kitsch trimmings inside.
Pay at the door and queue on the winding stair,
giving in the ticket torn to claim the twilight.

The bar is crushed. We get the wrong drinks and the right
change. And, yes, the touring band will play another hour
of cover versions, the girls wearing neon and ultra-violet,

scraps of cloth soon discarded, so many girls to dance
with, have a chance with; what the week has been waiting for —
sartorial ability, nervous instability, a cloaking device.

Yes, the bar: where we stand or lean or wobble and fall,
the ego fortified with the darkness and the drafts of beer
after the inevitable refusal, refusal and refusal;

the see-through walls of soap-flakes, mirrored stardust,
bottled ships, boiled sweets and the snug's drunken lair,
the Guinness atmosphere so thick you can cut it

and it heals itself against the optics emitting the only light,
an aristocracy of whiskey, when we order another round before
the bloated security jobsworths call time. And yes, though

our heads will surely break, the weekend starts here.

LAST LOOK

The old man asks for money
simply because you have taken his wife.
You refuse, and load another roll of Ektachrome.
These people are like kilometres —
again we're on the wrong side of the road.

After a late breakfast we leave
the scalding zinc-top and head down the oven
of the rental car, frowned upon by gawky geraniums
lining the awkward steps creased
like silver pillows below the Alhambra

tricked out in unfaltering light
and a good crick of the neck from our parking space.
Perspective makes a difference to our viewpoint
so we add it to our calculations,
and up we go, if only to see

how far we have come from the winter tiger
of the Sierra Nevada stalking this city and plain,
its striped haunches flexed to realign
the muscular snow. At which point,
like homesick Moors,

we agree that this last look is as seductive
as the first; except, when we look again,
the hermetic rooftops and tesserae of agriculture,
too late, it's already lost to us, the last province
to fall to the poor envious Christians.

FOR YOUR SINS

The busy-body telephonists,
the women in the library
or on the supermarket checkouts;
the redhead among the Woolworth's Pick 'n' Mix,
the Boots' brunette at the perfume counter,
the strawberry-blonde cashier
unfolding your modest cheques.

All very well,
but it's this one who's going to steal
the light from your eye
and put your foot to sleep,

the nasty girl with homemade contraceptives
and profitable in latex and wig,
a rubber corset, mask and lusty whip,
a steel stud through both sets of lips,
dagger heels
twenty minutes in the lacing-up...

Ordinarily she'd run a mile rather than go
for little you.

HOWARD WRIGHT is a lecturer in Art History at the University of Ulster,
Belfast. His last pamphlet collection was *Usquebaugh* (Redbeck Press,
Bradford 1997). He has reviews of Peter Reading's *Work in Regress* in
Brangle 3, and of Tom Paulin's *The Wind-Dog* in the current issue of
Magma. He currently has poems in *Writing Ulster*, *Stand*, *Thumbscrew*
and *HU*.

All Black

Michel Faber

'ARE WE THERE yet?'

My daughter's head stirs on my shoulder. Lulled by the thrum-da-dum-dum of the train, I have been dozing too. Daydreaming of John stroking the small of my naked back, his middle finger straying into the cleft of my bottom. I blink against the reality of this long journey away from him.

'Let me see my watch,' I say, shrugging my right arm under the weight of her warm little body. She moves just enough for me to get my wrist into view.

'Ages to go yet,' I say.

'But it's dark.'

'It just looks that way, 'cause the lights are on and the train windows are tinted.' It's an authoritative, grown-up explanation, but inside me I have my doubts. It really does look quite dark out there. I wonder if my watch is wrong.

'Are you hungry?'

She doesn't reply. Asleep again. My forearm has pins and needles now; I flex my hand, but carefully. If I move too much, my daughter will get irritable and shift her head from my shoulder to my lap. I can't afford to be seen with my daughter's head in my lap, even by total strangers on a train. If my wife heard about it, she'd accuse me of paedophilia, incest, child abuse, whatever. My access rights are hanging by a thread as it is.

Looking sideways, across the aisle, at the man flicking through the free railway magazine, I manage to read the digital numbers on his wristwatch. They're the same as on mine. Outside, it looks like sunset.

I rub my eyes with my left hand. My eyelids are still sore from all the crying. I am in transit between two people who are furious with me. I am travelling two hundred miles only to exchange one tantrum of hysterical jealousy for another.

My wife can't talk to me for two minutes without letting me know how much it hurts her to live on the same planet as me. We'll start off talking about Tess, what our daughter has or hasn't had to eat or drink, and almost immediately my wife will be shrieking, weeping, threatening, invoking the name of her lawyer. Weeks pass without me seeing Tess, and I have to get the woman at legal aid to write a letter for me, so that my wife doesn't bin it unread. Then finally we come to some arrangement. I can take Tess to McDonalds. Or the zoo. Or the movies. Two hundred miles' journey, and I pay to sit in a dark cinema with my daughter as she watches sentimental heterosexual garbage from the Walt Disney corporation.

When Tess is with her mother, which is almost every minute of my life, my partner John is happy. He doesn't mention her, pretends she doesn't exist. He sucks my cock as if it's never had any biological purpose except to give him pleasure. He revels in the freedom of unsafe sex with me, secure in the knowledge that I'm no risk. It's as if he's encoded my ten years of faithful marriage as a pre-sexual state, a kind of virginity preparing me for him. All we have to do is be inseparable from each other, and the plagues of the world can't touch us.

But when I talk about how much I miss my daughter, his face darkens. In a manner of speaking. John being black.

This visit, the first time Tessa has come to stay a weekend with me in my new home, has been hell. Hell for me, hell for John. I don't know what Tessa thought of it all. John didn't mention her name when he was shouting abuse and recriminations at me, as I was leaving. He was at least mature enough not to do that. He's growing older too, little by little. Soon — if we can get over this — the age difference between us will matter less and less.

Something is wrong with the train. It's slowing to a halt. The sky outside is grey, as if overcast, even though it's cloudless. The train stops.

'Are we there yet?'

'Nowhere near.'

'What's happening?'

'I don't know.'

The train starts moving backwards, smoothly and quietly. Tess sits up and presses her face and palms against the window, watching the trees and electricity poles going the wrong way.

An announcement comes over the PA. There is signalling failure up ahead, and the train is going back a few stops, to Perth. From there, passengers for Edinburgh and beyond will be conveyed by coach. Apologies, unavoidable, every effort being made, don't lumber us with your luggage.

'Are we going back to John's house?' Tessa asks, frowning.

'It's not John's house,' I retort without thinking. 'It's my house.'

She is silent. I am sick with misery. The greatest victory my wife can win is for every truly happy memory I have of me and our daughter to be locked in the past – the straight years. I'm not allowed to have any happy parenting memories that don't have my wife in them, as if all the wonderful moments (chasing the squealing toddler Tess around the garden with the watering can, balancing her on her tricycle, teaching her how to put new laces in her trainers) were only possible because Heather was standing by, approving.

'No, we're not going back,' I sigh. 'The train has to drop us off at a station. The special lights it needs to see the safe way home aren't working properly. We're going on a coach instead.'

'With horses?'

'No, coaches are… well, they're buses, basically.'

I know she's going to ask me what the difference is, and I'm racking my brains in the few seconds' grace.

'What's the difference between a coach and a bus?'

'I don't think there is one. It's like the difference between films and movies.'

John wouldn't like that, theatre director that he is. For him, films are uncompromising arty projects made by committed auteurs. Movies are Hollywood hamburgers. But there is a bigger world of language outside John's narrow queer one. It's not my world anymore, but it's there. And most people live in it.

'Has John got a job?' my daughter asks, as fearlessly as if she were asking if he owned a bicycle.

'I told you: he's a playwright. He writes plays.'

'Like *Peter Pan*?'

'No. For grown-ups. There was one being performed at a special festival just before we came up to visit.'

'What was it about?'

My mind goes blank when I think of John's play. At first I think this is because I'm stressed with the grief of him telling me we can't go on together, then I think it's because of how difficult it is to explain a gay play to a child so as not to make her mother go ballistic.

After a few more seconds, I realise it's neither of those things. In the lurid electric light of the train interior, travelling backwards with my eight-year-old daughter at my side, I suddenly realise that my gorgeous talented award-winning partner's play wasn't about anything really. It was just about being gay. Judged next to any children's story, it had no plot to speak of.

I take a deep breath.

'It was about... Somebody tries to get a person to give up being a politician.'

'How?'

'By telling a secret about him.'

'What secret?'

I snigger playfully, caught between fatherly tease and infantile embarrassment.

'It's a secret,' I wink.

'Can I see the play?' she says, rising to the challenge.

'It's over,' I tell her.

'Over?'

'It was on for a while,' I say, recalling the passions, the intrigues, the arguments, the complicated negotiations, that were poured into those ten long days. 'Then it closed.'

There is a pause while Tess chews this over.

'So everybody knows the secret except me,' she says at last.

'Yeah,' I grin, feeling dirty, as ashamed of my cowardice and my compromise as Tessa's mother would like me to feel of my sexuality itself.

The train is stopping at Perth station: more PA messages about not leaving anything behind. Tessa peers through the window at the descending gloom.

'Is it night time?' she says, as she gathers her things together.

'No, it's only afternoon. Four thirty.'

'Is it going to rain, then?'

I'm preoccupied with checking we have everything while people jostle past us through the aisle.

'I don't know. Maybe.'

'My carry bag is open at the top,' she reminds me. 'I don't want my new book to get wet.'

I am shocked by this concern of hers. Her new book is *Great People Through The Ages*, given her as a present by John when she first arrived — when he was still able to keep his feelings under wraps. I would've thought she'd want to dump the book in the nearest trash bin as soon as I wasn't looking. But she is frowning, trying to figure out a way of folding the top of her carry bag so it can't be rained on.

'It's all right, Tess, if it starts raining I'll shelter it inside my coat.' I am almost weeping again. This is what it's come to: tears I would once have shed over momentous events like the birth of a child or the death of a close relative I now want to shed when it looks as if there's some hope that my daughter will accept the gift of a crappy politically-correct book from my lover.

We step out onto the platform. All the lights are on. But then they always are, aren't they, in railway stations? I look beyond the concrete carapace of the glorified shed we've been stranded in. The sky is mauve now, and I am unsettled to discover that I can't tell whether the luminous orb near the horizon is the sun or the moon.

A uniformed employee of the railway is beckoning us towards the overpass stairs. He is holding a hastily felt-tipped sign that reads 'Edinburgh and The South', as if Edinburgh and The South were a rhythm & blues band struggling to draw a crowd at the local pub.

'This way,' I say, still choking on my hopes for a brighter future.

In the station car park, there are three coaches, or buses, waiting. One for Glasgow/Carlisle, one for Edinburgh/Newcastle, one for London. My daughter and I stand in the correct queue, along with about thirty other people. Immediately behind us, a young man and woman make the best of the circumstances by snogging. The sound of their lips sucking on each other is comically erotic and a bit surreal under the darkening sky. A middle-aged lady in front of us remarks on the strange weather.

'Not natural, is it?' she sniffs.

I feel perversely tempted to defend the rights of the sky to go dark whenever it pleases, but say nothing. I am on my way back to the straight world. There are rules to be obeyed. By the time I get to my wife's place in Keswick, I'll be so straight-acting someone's liable to try and sign me up to the local football team.

'John's a nice colour,' says Tessa all of a sudden. 'Nicer than I thought.'

I blush from my ears down to my shoulders. I wish we were alone in a room together, my daughter and I. Then I could sit back in an armchair while she said these things, and allow myself to go faint with pleasure at hearing them, without this sick fear of having to shush her any moment.

'Your mum already told you he was black, didn't she?' I remind her gently. The memory of Heather hissing at me, in front of Tess, that it must be a nice change for me to play with a big black dick instead of my own limp little excuse, is still raw in my mind.

'He doesn't look black to me,' says Tessa. 'He's brown'.

I smile. Black people are something of a rarity in my wife's town. Invisible, almost. Like homosexuals. They only exist when they're arrested or in trouble.

'We say he's black, though,' I inform her. 'That's just the way it is.'

Tess is not to be fobbed off in this way.

'But he's *not*,' she insists. 'He's... he's the colour of chocolate blancmange.'

I burst out laughing. The thought of John as a sculpture of chocolate blancmange makes him ridiculous and benign. A little less like a fearsome, formless chaos of emotions, capable of sweeping me out of his life like a natural disaster. I think of the surface of refrigerated blancmange as it returns to room temperature: the silky dusting of condensation slowly starting to twinkle. I think of John's skin. But Tessa is still waiting for a satisfactory explanation.

'We use the word black because he's not white like us,' I offer.

'We're not white,' she says, as if any fool could see this.

'Well, close enough,' I sigh.

'You're *pink*,' she tells me, pointing up at my face. 'With red spots. And in the dark, you're black. We're all black.'

We are finally allowed to board the bus, coach, whatever. It's five o'clock by now but looks like eight. Just about all the light in the sky is gone. There are no stars, and the moon — yes, it definitely must have been the moon I saw — is pale.

As soon as we've taken our seats, Tess switches on the overhead light, the little directional one next to the ventilation nub. She extracts John's book from her carry bag and opens it at page one.

The bus driver apologises on behalf of the train company for the delay, and reminds us that there is to be no smoking anywhere on the vehicle. He will drive us to each of the railway stations the train would have stopped at, except for the 'really out-of-the-way ones.' Anyone from such a station is invited to come forward and make a special request. No one comes forward. We are all normal, no trouble.

The bus pulls out of the car park, its headlights sweeping across the gloomy tarmac. On our way to the main road, a few drunken-looking young men wave, but by and large the streets of Perth seem deserted. It's as if people have hurried home in anticipation of the downpour or the snowstorm or whatever it is that is threatening in the skies.

On the seat next to me, Tess is reading about the great men and women of history. A very butch-looking Sappho is on the same page as Shakespeare, but little Tess isn't quite ready for poetry yet. She turns pages until she finds Cleopatra, who is as black-skinned as, well, a chocolate blancmange. The Nile Queen sits in a throne flanked by handmaidens and exotic pets. There seem to be no men in this particular nook of ancient Egypt.

I wonder why I'm so irritated by this book, given that these people did exist, and were most likely as black and/or as gay as they're painted here. Isn't this better than the history books I grew up with, full of macho white men fighting wars? At random, I read a bit of the text. It says that Cleopatra was a wise and resourceful ruler who did all she could to prevent her peaceable civilisation falling into the hands of greedy Roman plunderers. I somehow suspect that in this book, Cleopatra is not going to spread her legs for any hunky man in armour.

'What does mummy say about John and me?' I ask Tess once the bus has been travelling for a while.

'Nothing,' says Tess.

'Nothing at all?'

'She's busy.'

'Busy taking care of you?'

'Just busy.'

Defeated, I look out the window. Even allowing for the tinted windows, it's bizarrely dark out there. At a time of evening when, only yesterday, it was barely dusk. Car headlights flash past us monotonously. The bus driver murmurs into a mobile phone. Time passes.

I become aware that the people travelling in the bus with us are very quiet. I hear a couple of them whisper to each other from time to time, but otherwise nobody says anything. I swivel around in my seat, to take stock of my fellow passengers. They glance back at me, startled, white-faced. No, *really* white-faced. They are afraid. They, too, remember yesterday. They, too, can't see any reason why today should be so different.

As we drive on, we go slower and slower. The driver frequently flashes his headlights in warning to approaching cars. It seems some motorists haven't accepted the freakish weather conditions and are driving without lights, as if visibility was fine. As if they refuse to be bullied by what they see as an unreasonable change in the prevailing conditions. Alarmingly, the darker the sky gets, the more motorists seem to be in the grip of this wishful thinking.

'Jesus, wake up, will you?' mutters our driver loudly, as another unlit car hurtles past us like a missile.

Pretty soon we are travelling at thirty miles an hour. Every fourth or fifth vehicle we pass has no lights on. Some of them hoot their horns mournfully, most just pootle by in silence.

With so little illumination outside, the windows of the bus become mirrors. Each of us stares uneasily at his or her reflected chiaroscuro face. Except Tess, who keeps reading her new book. The great 'woman of colour' Harriet Tubman is freeing the slaves, with a little help from an unpictured president.

'Interesting book?' I ask, clearing my throat first.

'Uh-huh,' she replies. She reaches up to the air-conditioning nozzle and fiddles with it. I can tell she's mistaken this nozzle for a dimmer, and is trying to make her light shine stronger.

'That's for air,' I tell her gently. 'The light isn't adjustable. It's either on or off.'

'It's getting darker,' she complains.

'Yes,' I say, squinting out of the window.

'No,' she says, 'not out there. In *here*. The *light* is getting darker.'

She points to the book on her lap. A female astronaut is smiling for a photograph taken shortly before she's blown to atoms in the *Challenger*. I can barely make out the text. My daughter is right.

Before long the light inside the bus is fading to a submarine luminescence. The engine still purrs obediently, but it's as if all the cabin bulbs are connected to their own little batteries, batteries that happen to be running down at the same time. The overhead lights, the light above the first-aid compartment, the light for whether the closet toilet is occupied or not: all dimming to yellow. It occurs to me that having a toilet is probably what makes a coach different from a bus, but now is not the time to raise this educational fact with Tessa. I'm glad she's engrossed in her book of great people, oblivious to the mounting tension.

A woman makes her way up the aisle and alerts the driver to what he can see perfectly well for himself. He answers her irritably. She returns to her seat, and passes on the message to her husband in an anxious whimper. He mutters loud reassurances to her, like 'Bollocks,' 'We'll see about that,' and so on.

'Get a fuckin' move on!' someone shouts from the very back.

The driver speaks tersely to someone on his little telephone. Then, cursing under his breath, he rotates the steering wheel vigorously and veers us off the road.

The coach cruises on a bay of smooth bitumen, finally coming to rest in front of a petrol station. At least I *think* it's a petrol station. Yes: I can just make out the filling pumps standing in shadow, like blasted tree stumps. There is a pale rectangle of light further on, emanating from the glass front of the station building itself. I can see several people standing close together in there, huddled behind the counter, illuminated by a single flickering phosphorescent tube.

The coach door swings open with a hiss. As soon as our driver rears up from his seat and steps out of the coach, I know, deep in my guts, right inside my bone marrow, that my daughter and I have to get out too. All around us, our heavy-breathing, shadowy fellow-passengers are seething with panic, hesitating on the nightmare brink between passivity and mania.

'Come on, Tess, we're going.'

Amazingly, she doesn't protest that we're not there yet, or ask questions. She just dumps her book in her carry bag and scrambles out into the aisle. I don't even bother with my own bag, which has my underwear and dressing gown in it, my dressing gown which always smells of the man I love. I push Tessa along with both hands, and we jump out of the bus like we're leaping off a spinning merry-go-round.

The driver is already arguing heatedly with the people through the locked glass door of the service station, but whatever he is arguing with them about becomes irrelevant when the engine of his bus suddenly roars without him. Gears squealing, the vehicle lurches out of the parking bay. Its head and tail lights die as it speeds onto the road, making it look less like a bus than a trailer-load of dark metal being towed by an invisible force.

I scoop Tess up in my arms and run clumsily after it. Not to catch up with the bus, just to get back to the road. I must reach the open road, I don't know why, I just must. My daughter weighs a ton, struggling and squirming, trying to evade the sharpness of my fingers against her ribs.

'I can run, Daddy,' she pants, so I put her down. Behind us at the service station, a crash of glass is followed by shouts and screams. Tess and I sprint through the darkness, through a miasma of diesel fumes.

A few minutes later, we're standing by the side of a motorway. Not on a slip road: on the fine-gravelled edge of the actual motorway itself. There are large signs warning that this is illegal, but those signs are shrouded in shadow. Only about a third of the motorway lamps have any light coming out of them at all, and the glow is so feeble that it's affected by insects flying round the glass. The sky is inky black, without stars. A sinking moon is diffused like an acid burn against the horizon, subtly outlining the edges of city buildings — an extinguished city.

'I'll get you home, Tess,' I promise, as three dark cars whizz past us.

Tessa takes no interest in the traffic; she's looking at me, chewing at her lips. There's something she needs to say, some vital piece of information she feels I can no longer be expected to cope without.

'Mummy sleeps with all the lights on,' she says, staring at me as if this knowledge is sure to knock me flat. 'Every room in the house. All lit up. I switch mine off when she's gone to sleep.'

Of course I haven't the faintest idea how to take this. I smile gravely and nod as if I understand, just like I do with John when he's raging against enemies who seem quite harmless to me, just like I used to do with my wife when she'd try to tell me what a woman needs.

A car with headlights blazing speeds into view. I stick my thumb out, then wave frantically with my whole hand. The car doesn't even slow down, and I almost get my arm slammed off by its passenger mirror.

'Don't get run over, Daddy!' pleads my daughter. Actually, it's more of a command, and I feel her fist seizing the fabric of my coat.

I stand well back, and wait for the next lighted car. Twenty, thirty dark ones pass. Some of them are badly dented, some have unidentifiable smears and splatters on their bodywork. One driver winds down a window and yells something we cannot hear, but other than this the cars might as well be empty shells.

In between rejections, the motorway is as still and lonely as a canyon. I wonder how long all this is taking, and look at my watch. The electronic numbers have disappeared, leaving my watch a useless bracelet.

Time can now only be measured in the gradual dimming of the motorway lamps. A huge articulated lorry stops for us just as the last of them is petering out. We can't quite believe it as it approaches, a monstrous filthy thing crawling along in the slow lane with its grid of headlights on dazzling full beam. It comes to a standstill right next to us, a balm of heat and diesel radiating from its greasy undercarriage. The driver's cabin is so high off the ground we can't see anyone inside. For a few moments we stand staring.

'Well, do you want a fucking lift or not?' a hoarse male voice calls out.

I jolt into action, wresting the cabin door open, trying to lift Tess up onto a metal rung. She slips out of my grasp, climbing like a monkey, leaving me holding her carry bag. I scramble after her, banging a shin in my haste, in my fear that some unknown man is going to drive my daughter away into the dark.

As soon as we're inside, before I've even slammed the door shut, we're on the move.

'Thanks,' I say, suppressing a coughing fit in the thick haze of cigarette smoke.

'No probs,' says the driver. He is a giant of a man, like a bodybuilder gone to seed, ugly but mesmerising. His grey hair is slicked with oil, his shovel-shaped face is ruddy and bristled. He keeps his bloodshot eyes on the road as he speaks.

'Get off of my gear stick,' he says. Tessa moves her legs closer to mine. We squash together, father and daughter.

'Where you going?' he says, as he overtakes two unlit cars. I note that he flips on his indicators while doing this, as if light were in plentiful supply.

'I… my daughter's going home to her mother's. In Keswick.'

'Where the fuck's that?'

'It's in Cumbria.'

'I ain't going to fucking Cumbria. I'm going to the depot.'

'Where's the depot?'

'Carlisle.'

I don't know what to say, so I say, 'Fine.' Carlisle is not a million miles away from where I'm trying to get to, except that I have no idea anymore where I should be heading for. My wife's house may be hidden in pitch darkness by now. John's house — my house — may be the same. All I want is to find a little oasis of light where I can get my daughter safely settled.

'Do you think there'll be light at the depot?'

'There fucking better be.'

'And if there's not?'

'I'll soon get it sorted.'

His self-possession is inspirational, irritating, terrifying, sexy. I want to grab him by the sleeve and ask him what the hell he thinks is happening. I'm afraid to ask, even politely, in case he says he doesn't know, in case he suddenly starts weeping and wailing, this big strong man with his arms like Arnold Schwarzenegger. I want to leave his confidence unchallenged, surrender myself to his agenda, cling to the light he trusts in so blindly.

A wave of nausea passes over me and I realise that I haven't slept in a long time. Instead, I've spent the weekend nights arguing in my lover's bed, defending the right of humankind to propagate itself, begging for a kiss, inventing preposterous conspiracy theories as to why a perfectly good and popular play should be pulled off the stage after ten performances. If I make it as far as Heather's house, she's hardly likely to greet me with pillows and blankets. I tilt my head back and count to ten and beyond.

The driver seems more interested in Tessa than in me. Possibly he has a little daughter too, or happy memories of one.

'Past your bedtime, eh?' he smirks out of the side of his mouth.

'It's still early,' says Tess. She is quite capable of reading the time on the glowing dashboard clock.

'Right enough, right enough,' grins the driver. 'Where you been, then?'

'Visiting.'

'Very good.'

'My dad's friend gave me a book.'

'Very nice.'

'Can I have the light on?' she asks, pointing to the switch for the cabin bulb.

He shakes his head.

'Not while I'm driving. It's against the law. I could get done for it.'

She folds her arms across her chest, miffed. The three of us sit not speaking for a while, perched on top of the giant motor growling and vibrating through the floor. I look out the window. From my high vantage point, I have a good view of the countryside, especially now that the motorway lamps are all off. To my bewilderment, I can see that there are still houses and buildings, dotted here and there across the benighted landscape, in which lights are glowing just like normal. Every now and then, we drive close by a village or a town, and I can see beacons — a single functioning street light, an illuminated church clock, even a shop sign — shining mysteriously in the almost universal gloom. There seems no logic to it, no reason why.

Our driver is ready for another cigarette. He steers with his elbows while he attempts, unsuccessfully, to strike a match. Three matches fall dead on the floor before he gives up and tosses the box away. But there is a cigarette lighter in his dashboard, and he uses that. His cigarette tip glows fierce and bright as he sucks hard on the filter.

Tess is fidgeting, slumping, shoring herself up again, sinking towards unconsciousness. Gingerly she rests her cheek on the back of the seat and blinks into the invisible cargo hidden behind a veil of steel mesh.

'What's in the back?' she says.

'Stuff,' the driver replies.

'What stuff?'

'It's a secret.'

She sighs and goes to sleep. The driver catches my eye and winks. Then he stretches his back, gyrates his massive shoulders, cracks his knuckles, and settles down to drive us through the long night.

MICHEL FABER's first collection of short stories, *Some Rain Must Fall* won the Saltire Scottish First Book of the Year award in 1999, and his novel *Under the Skin* was critically acclaimed and is due to be published in the USA shortly by Harcourt Brace. He is currently working on another novel for Canongate.

Mrs Mahmood

S.A. Afolabi

ISOBEL AND I live above the route of an underground line. We hadn't been told this before we moved in so it came as a shock the first time the 6.25 rumbled beneath our heads. Isobel thought it might be an earthquake. I knew exactly what it was. My heart sank. Now, sometimes I lie awake at night waiting for another train to pass so that I can fall asleep: I find it comforting somehow. The regularity, the mild vibrations, the dim, distant thrum of carriages carrying other people elsewhere. I couldn't live in a quiet place now. My tolerance for tranquillity has gone.

In the sports shop where I work it's noisy too; it can quite often seem overwhelming. We aren't large area-wise. We have a high concentration of stock. Also, being near the university is a boon during term time. It gets busy, and I prefer that to sparse custom.

What happened the other week should not have come as a surprise. Deborah was serving on the cash till. I was balanced on a ladder, rehanging the tracksuit bottoms, smoothing them down where people had thrown them back haphazardly. Cedric was serving a boy of about thirteen, helping him choose a pair of running shoes. Nike. Size nine.

I shifted the ladder to another section of the shop. I think a clean, immaculate appearance is the essence of a caring, responsible enterprise. It sends out a message beyond the doors: Experience and Understanding you will find here. That's what I believe in. Understanding. It's what I strive for.

They don't like me doing this, the other staff, the rinse and interference of it. I think they would prefer me out the back taking care of the accounts, harrying suppliers, rushing in new stock. I don't know this for certain. I'm the manager, I should have mentioned. Perhaps it puts them on edge, as if I am constantly watching, scrutinising. But that isn't my priority. I'm just particular about order, things running in straight lines. Dust doing a disappearing act. Perhaps I get this from my wife.

I wasn't paying particular attention to what was happening in the shop. I tend to run on automatic pilot when I'm doing the mundane tasks. That way I can free my mind to concentrate on improvements, long-term plans. The boy with the trainers was wandering around the shop floor, testing out the shoes. He walked a few metres, stopped, then reached up on his toes. Sometimes I'll look at the young, wonder whether they are headed for great things. This one seemed to soar like a gazelle, he didn't waver on his feet. Then he crouched down low, stood up again and made his way back to the chair. I like that in a customer, someone who really knows what he wants. Someone who can pick out strengths and weaknesses and isn't afraid to do so in the setting of the shop. A lot of people are quite shy. They'll wear a pair of shoes, stand up, sit down, then immediately say, Yes, I'll take these. They might look flushed, a little sheepish, as if they've caused an inconvenience, put out a member of staff. Often I'll want to say something to them. Ask them to walk around a bit, deliberate. But I don't say anything of course; it's money in the till after all.

Cedric asked the boy some questions, went through the usual routine about the feel of them, what they'd be used for. The boy looked down at the shoes and scrunched his feet a bit. He wore a slight grimace as if he couldn't quite make up his mind. There was another boy then. I don't know where he appeared from, but he had been inside the shop all along. He called out for some assistance and Cedric moved to help him. It occurred to me to step down from the ladder, to assist, but then I did not.

Without a moment's hesitation, the boy in the trainers walked out of the shop. He didn't run or look behind himself or suddenly tear off down the street. He walked away as if he had been wearing his own shoes, walking out of his own house. I watched impassively. By the time I had reached the door, he was some way down Tottenham Court Road. I started to run. He glanced around, noticed me, and then he began to sprint. There were pedestrians about, tackling their Christmas shopping. I like this time of day because people seem less brusque; they're more relaxed. The hard, brittle city edge that coats the beginning of the day has worn down.

Perhaps it is an odd sight to see an older man puffing down a street. The clumsy sweep and sway of it, the heavy body bounding along. All I know is that very few people were looking at the boy, but all eyes managed to fix on me. Paths cleared. People stood back. It may have been an alarming sight.

When I was seventeen, I took a coach to Hastings. There were thirty of us on board. There was an athletics meeting between four or five schools and we all knew this occasion was important. Gold medals in any event might lead to county representation. Our athletics instructor Mr. Mayers paced the coach, dispensing pep talks, trying to steel our morale.

The track at the school in Hastings was new, better than anything we had previously used. This was a school where no one thought anything of flying abroad for the half-term. Most of the other competitors had arrived before us. They looked polished, almost professional as we straggled off the coach. My stomach yapped a little, then growled and I could feel my lunch lurch.

As the start drew near, we poured on to the field, talking, stretching, warming up. A group from another school turned to look at us, then folded in amongst themselves like bats. My picture once appeared in the local newspaper. And then there were some sentences in the gazette. It was no secret that I'd broken a string of county records for my age group the previous year. I hung medals and certificates on the walls at school. I talked incessantly of my own prowess. I make no apology for this, either now or then: I used to think it was an essential ingredient of success. I could envisage my life stretching out ahead of me, consisting of adulation and accomplishment in equal measure.

Thirty minutes into the games and it was clear we had serious competition. People were not even qualifying in the heats. Suddenly it seemed to me that the bar on the high jump was insurmountable, distances on the field too arduous. I felt tired in a way I had never experienced before. Not from fatigue or from running too hard. It was simply exhausting to watch success slip so quickly away.

There comes a time when you realise that all the effort you've put in — all those early mornings, the rigorous diet, the training, pushing yourself to the limit — amounts to nothing. I told friends I would return the next year, invigorated. I convinced myself of that at the time. But I never picked up another pair of running shoes, never stepped on to another track.

I don't think the boy ever guessed I would catch up with him. He probably thought he could shake me, an old dog giving up the chase. But I caught him all right. I could tell he was shocked: he didn't say a word. He didn't struggle. Halfway back to the shop we met Cedric. There was a queue of traffic alongside us. The air was beginning to thin in the onslaught of winter darkness.

I caught a glimpse of the other boy lurking behind a pillar. I realised then that he had been a decoy. I cannot describe how I felt then. Cheated? Flummoxed? Enraged? All three?

Cedric told him to take off the shoes. There were unsaleable now. The boy slipped them off nonchalantly, kicked them to one side. Then he began to put on his own worn-out trainers. I should have noted that from the beginning: no-one enters a shoe shop wearing decrepit shoes. I've noticed that. The boy sat there, saturnine, bored, as if this happened every other day. When I said I would call the police, his expression did not change. I don't know what I was expecting. Remorse? Something, anything to let me know he had registered regret. But that didn't happen. Not after my threat to resort to the law or my rising tone of voice or Cedric's more temperate approach. The boy's face just expressed contempt.

You could say I lost my temper. I could feel the held rage seeping from my chest, like a disturbed wound. I raised my hand, then slowly brought it down again and scratched the back of my neck. I was ready to strike out. The boy didn't even cringe. He showed no emotion whatsoever. I don't like to see that in children, coldness, valves already shut off. Perhaps that's exactly what he expected. Quite possibly he'd been struck before.

It's a good thing we haven't any children, Isobel and I. I can't abide surly behaviour. I'm just the sort of person who could so easily lose control.

Cedric told me to cool off. Deborah led me back to the office, like an invalid. When I sat down my hands were trembling, the knuckles doing some kind of dance. In the end, the boy's mother was contacted. She apologised, even paid for the shoes, and thanked the staff for not alerting the police. That's what Cedric told me the next day. I left early. Though that's not something I often do.

I drove to the supermarket, bought sea bass, mineral water and a bottle of white wine. For once I'd arrived home before Isobel and I wanted to surprise her. Also, I needed something to do with my hands, to keep myself occupied. I turned the music up loud, opened the wine and started on that. Isobel doesn't drink during the week. She says it impairs her judgment, her reasoning, and she likes to keep her mind clear. She's an orthoptist at a children's hospital, not that it would make any difference to her work.

I heard the door shut. Then the music was turned down so that it was almost inaudible.

'Turn it back up,' I shouted. I was still simmering. I walked into the living room, a glass of wine in one hand, a bowl of steaming white rice in the other. She was lingering by the stereo, wearing her long beige coat, her bag limp over her shoulder. I waved the bowl about so that steam plumed into the air. It was supposed to be a jovial gesture. She took one good look at me.

'What's wrong?' she said.

I shrugged and sauntered back into the kitchen. 'Time to eat!' I called.

In Isobel's work with the children, she often gets to see a side to life that I'm unaware of. Sometimes she strikes a tone with me that isn't appropriate. 'Now then,' she might say quietly, 'tell me all about it.' Her hands held gently together, her voice smooth, modulated. I know she'd like children of our own, but me, I'm not so sure.

I explained what had happened during the day. The shoes marching out defiantly, the high-street chase, how I'd wanted to lash out. I've always thought of myself as a particular kind of man, the kind that could never strike a child. No matter what. But that's all over now.

Isobel made a few cooing noises. I didn't know what she meant. She gathered up the dishes and walked into the kitchen. She was wearing a batik wrapround the colour of blueberries swirled in yoghurt, a white T-shirt and an oversized tan cardigan. You could say that Isobel is stunning and you would not be exaggerating. I could hear the hot tap gushing, the basin filling up with suds. When she returned, I was in the middle of pouring the last of the wine.

'Well, Mr Mahmood,' she shrugged, but she didn't sound upset. 'Theft is something you just have to get used to. I thought you'd be used to it by now?'

'Theft?' I repeated. 'I'm not worried about that,' I said, even though I have always been.

I explained again about the insolent boy. I thought she might be shocked. 'Oh that! That's nothing new,' she said. 'I've sometimes wanted to hit out, you know. You can't help that.'

I nibbled the edge of my glass.

'It's only natural to feel anger at that kind of behaviour,' she continued. 'They're doing it for a reason, though. You have to remember that.'

I wasn't quite sure how to take this, the ease with which she'd said it. I stood up and the table swam before me. I was a bit drunk — I'm not often that way — I just couldn't settle down. I placed the rest of the crockery into Isobel's foamy bath. I could feel my muscles aching already from my mid-afternoon sprint.

I picked up the car keys and announced I was going for a drive. She immediately grabbed them off me and said, 'Let's go' as I knew she would.

We decided to visit the hill in order to walk off the alcohol. The evening was slick with fresh-fallen drizzle and as soon as we reached Elsworthy Road neither of us was in the mood to leave the warmth of the car. Instead we carried on, through Camden and then to the centre of town to look at the lights along Bond Street. Isobel was driving slowly. She didn't want to miss a thing.

'I just have to go there,' she kept pointing to particularly expensive shops.

'Yes,' I said, agreeing too quickly. I felt nauseous. I opened the window a crack and leaned up against the door. Isobel looked across at me. 'Eyes on the road, please,' I snapped. By the time we reached Piccadilly, I felt calmer, more refreshed.

Isobel, I think, was led to expect an undemanding life. To have things provided easily, frequent trips around the world. I don't think she ever envisaged being with someone like me. It must have come as a surprise, gone against everything her parents had encouraged her towards, to suddenly find on her wedding day, me and not some high-flown tycoon exchanging the marital vows. I know her mother was crestfallen. It wasn't difficult to notice that. Mr Hamilton put on a brave face, but in the beginning none of that mattered to us. Young love, as they often say, is blind. Life in a warm milky sea.

Perhaps it was the mother, her insistence. Dreams she had always aspired to, and been let down, so she turned to Isobel. I'm only speculating. Perhaps I'm way off the mark. My mother used to say, when she was living, that it didn't matter who you loved, what you did in this world as long as there was a little happiness in it.

I used to get annoyed at Isobel because sometimes she would remind me of her mother. Her distrusts, her exactitude, the way she held herself so stiffly when I wanted her simply to let go. The way she turned from certain things — music, say or people, raised voices — because they seemed to crowd the light. Who and what she thought she ought to be.

There was a time fraught with difficulties, when I wasn't sure what we were doing. But that's passed. I fought for Isobel, the way I've fought for most things in my life. I know she didn't want me in the beginning. Not for a long time after that.

We'll catch a bus sometimes, a train, discover a part of town or the country we've never been to before. Occasionally we've caught the wrong train, a bus going in the opposite direction. But there won't be any panic, a rushing towards the exit. Quite often we'll remain seated and let the vehicle lead the way. Isobel doesn't mind this, although I know she would never allow such a thing to happen on her own.

Like me, she's lived in other places — Guadalupe, Martinique, New York City after that — so she doesn't mind the travelling. Perhaps it comes from living a fractured existence. All that broken geography. Learning to live a different life.

Isobel once said I was abrupt with people, I cut them off, that underneath a warm exterior I harboured a cold nature.

'When?' I demanded. 'When am I like this? Examples please.'

'Oh, I don't know,' she laughed. 'All the time, really. In a way.'

At the back of my mind I feared she was thinking about wanting children again, but she didn't mention it. I think a part of what she was saying has something to do with living in the city. I often strike a particular note with people and I can't say why. The sales representatives, for example, who come into the shop. Sometimes I make them feel as if they are the most important encounter of my day. That what they are saying bears close attention. What they are doing is admirable. At the end of it all — the bright photographs showing technicoloured shoes, leotards, samples of baseball caps, something that's happened in their day, their lives — there comes a point when they realise they have done all the talking. They're all talked out. And all I have given of myself is the minimum, the bare bones, while I know everything that has happened to them, all the dry reality of their day. Sometimes there will be a moment when they realise this. It's awkward because it's a signal to me that they might want something in exchange, muscle, blood, a heart, something more vibrant. And I know that there isn't any of that, only bones. Does that make me cold?

My customers, on the other hand, I treat as if we'll meet again. That's a favourite part of my job, the interaction, so I try to get it right. People don't like to admit they don't know, that they might need some help. I've learned that over time, so I've asked the staff to approach them in a particular manner — not invasive or aggressive — so that it puts them at ease. People don't like to feel crowded. There is a kind of satisfaction in watching them select an item, try something on. I love it when they walk out with bags of shopping in their hands, contented. Or the ones who ask demurely if they can wear the shoes out of the shop.

That happened today, this afternoon. Someone came into the shop. Someone famous. I'd seen him during the summer on my television screen. He wasn't shopping for himself; he had a young boy with him, most probably his son.

I let Deborah do the talking, make the sale, do all of that. He bought a pair of football boots, not the best I noted. It was the boy's choice.

They were warm people, relaxed. I watched them from where I stood, half-heartedly checking the stock. They smiled along with Deborah. The boy kept giggling. His father laughed out loud. A few customers sidled up for autographs. He was in the last Olympics, that one. An Olympian. He had a winner's smile.

At one stage, he caught me looking and I turned away. I think I lost my nerve then. I don't remember, I just felt weak. I fled into the office and sat staring at the paperwork. Half an hour may have passed. I thought I should telephone Isobel at the hospital. 'Who?' she would say. 'Which Olympics?'

Instead I slipped out of the building. It was wrong of me; I wouldn't tolerate that kind of behaviour in anyone else.

It was cold outside, but bright and windless. People moved less briskly in the streets, the reality of the new year setting in. I walked to Charing Cross with the intention of turning back. But then I just kept moving.

Along Whitehall, a bus waited patiently for its passengers to alight. It was stationary when I caught up with it and so, without hesitating, I stepped on. I didn't check where it was going. I just wanted to go and go and go, be carried somewhere far away.

It is a helpless feeling to know that no matter how hard you run, however much you exert yourself, you are never going to move faster than this, overtake the man in front. Perhaps I understood that then, when I was seventeen. I could have, in a minor way, grasped something early on: that there is a moment or a series of moments in life when you must wear a different pair of shoes, walk in another direction from the one you had planned, and however well you succeed in your pursuits, there will always be an element of regret.

The bus shuddered across the river. A refuse container made its sluggish progress beneath the bridge. I got off at the next stop and crossed the road into the park. It surprised me to see people there in the middle of the week, in the cold. I left the path after a while and slipped on to the field. There were some children at one end playing at the long jump. I walked around the perimeter slowly and I could hear their laughter. The track seemed warm and buoyant beneath me. There were signs — paint peeling off wooden benches, sections of the track torn out — of decay and neglect. The trees in the distance rustled slightly, but I did not feel the breeze.

I don't know why I behaved the way I did, that day in the shop with the thief. He had looked so angry with me. As if *I* had been in the wrong. What if Cedric hadn't been there? Would I have just struck out? I'd like to think not, but I'm not so certain of that now. Sometimes I think I take better care of my shop — the expensive shoes, the labelled clothing, the sports equipment — than I would my own child. That scares me a little.

I took off my jacket, laid it down to one side of the field. I stretched my limbs slowly, deliberately, the way I had been taught, because at my age things can so easily go wrong. I took up position and cast my eye to the end of the track. The children had stopped what they were doing. They were quiet now. Watching. And then I was sailing, the wind unfurling around my ears, the soft rubber track making me feel supple. As I neared the end of the straight I didn't stop as I'd intended, but instead, rounded the bend and ran at a slower pace back to the start. When I finished, there was a faint applause and when I looked up, there were the children in the distance who must have been cheering me on. I hadn't heard them. I'd heard nothing except the wind and my quick heartbeat, my laboured breath.

Perhaps I have failed in my life, in my endeavours. Perhaps the meaning of it all has passed me by. I can't say for certain that it has. I just don't know. I can't say that in a year from now I'll be lulled to sleep by underground trains. I could be someplace very far from here. Sometimes I long for the heat.

If it came right down to it, if I thought about it clean out, pared back the skin, the tired flesh and arrived at the bones, I realise the one certainty in my life is Isobel.

S.A. AFOLABI was born in Nigeria, and grew up in various countries including Canada, the Congo, Japan and Indonesia. He studied at Cardiff University, currently works at the BBC and has had fiction published in several magazines. He has recently completed a first novel.

Reviving critique

Ronald Turnbull

SCOTLAND ENTERS a new millennium, with our parliament only recently restored: an appropriate time and context, surely, for a wide-ranging and radical debate about the condition of Scottish society, and its future. Yet, as some commentators have observed, there have so far been few signs that any such public discussion will take place. The recent claim by Iain MacWhirter in *The Sunday Herald* that Scotland is in a state of 'intellectual torpor' may be hyperbolic, but he is right to note a disinclination to reflect seriously on 'where we are in the world, and what kind of society we want to be part of.'

Attempts to initiate a comprehensive and critical debate face major, seemingly insurmountable barriers. Both complacency and cynicism are deep-rooted and widespread in the culture, and these fuel a generalised hostility to ideas and critical thought. A further obstacle is the prevalence of the belief that, after the demise of socialism, there is in fact no longer any place for debate over fundamental issues, and no possibility of serious ideological conflict. It is assumed that meaningful public debate is now essentially pragmatic, discussion concerned with identifying the means which most efficiently and effectively deliver the goods (since — it is also assumed — we all know what the goods actually are).

The only substantial recently published work dedicated to discussion of Scotland's future testifies to the current dominance of an anti-theoretical, conformist and pragmatist ethos. Although advertised as 'the most ambitious and comprehensive analysis of Scotland in a generation,' and 'a timely critique of much of what passes for conventional wisdom in Scottish public life,' Gerry Hassan and Chris Warhurst's *A Different Future* is a collection of largely uncritical essays of limited focus. For instance, it contains calls for 'racial inclusion' and for more female representation in the ranks of Scottish entrepreneurs — however worthy, these can hardly be described as radical demands, nor do they qualify as challenges to conventional wisdom. It is revealing of the editors' approach that a number of the contributors are experts in such fields as business studies and marketing (disciplines which, whatever value they may possess, are not noted as sources of wide-ranging and critical social analysis), whereas there are no contributions from philosophers, historians or — dare it be said — theologians, those academics who, some might think, are most likely to be capable of taking an enlarged view of things, and of questioning received ideas. However, some of the essays broach or at least suggest matters with which a genuinely comprehensive and radical debate would have to be concerned.

Lindsay Paterson expresses the hope that, in the new Scottish politics, a 'radical questioning' of civic Scotland (or local elites) will take place, and that 'radical dissent' will become more vocal. It would be interesting to know what form he thinks such dissent could take. Would it be restricted to relatively fragmented, 'single-issue' projects, as his examples suggest — demands for community land ownership, and the commitment of some teachers to 'a vision of education as liberation'? More should have been said too about the important idea of voluntary social action, and the kind of philosophy on which it would be based. It is odd that Paterson believes the concept should be most congenial to Conservatives: surely the sense of social responsibility required for such action runs counter to a culture of individualism, and would itself therefore be a vital form of 'radical dissent'?

An essay by the intellectual heavyweight among the contributors, Tom Nairn, proposes one answer to the question about sources of dissent and critique. 'Redness lives!' he insists, while delivering a (disappointingly muffled) rebuke to ex-comrade Brown. But one can sympathise with Nairn's refusal to join Brown on his march along 'a road laid down by Thatcherite Conservatism,' and fully agree with him that a priority of the new Scottish politics must be to reduce inequalities, while at the same time doubting whether the Marxist-socialist traditions could still provide a viable basis for any popular or effective political project. Other considerations aside, they are simply too tainted by association with the failures and crimes of previously existing socialist projects.

Nonetheless, it is true that much of the Marxist and Frankfurt School analysis and moral critique of capitalism not only remains valid, but has actually acquired greater cogency. We inhabit a culture which fosters greed and self-advancement as primary human motives. Most employment denies workers the opportunity to fulfil their potential, so that work is generally seen as a means to acquisition and consumption, rather than activity directed towards the attainment of goods of excellence. Techniques designed to manipulate thought and behaviour are becoming more sophisticated and widespread. And, contrary to the claims of its imponents and ideologues, consumer capitalism increasingly generates, not personal autonomy and individuality, but a heteronomous uniformity of belief, discourse and desire.

What is more, over the past two decades there has been a remarkable intensification of class warfare, in the form of aggressive *Klassenkampf von oben*. Witness the extension of economic inequality; the undermining of trade union power; the normalisation of insecurity in employment; increased pressure on employees and the creation of a workplace 'culture of fear'; the more authoritarian treatment of the underclass by the state; and so on.

The public discourse of New Labourism, which informs many of the contributions to *A Different Future*, cannot of course acknowledge these grim truths, and has to contradict, deny, or obfuscate them. Thus, class struggle has been declared a thing of the past; 'social justice' is, as one contributor puts it, one of New Labour's 'most revered values'; we now all belong to a 'community,' or even 'caring community,' not a brutally competitive, and brutalising social system; the ideal of 'social inclusion' conveys the message that all that is amiss with society is that some are excluded from it. (See N. Fairclough's *New Labour, New Language?* (London: 2000), for a full critical analysis of New labour discourse.)

The claim that New Labour is committed to social justice plays a key role in its rhetoric, and calls for a little more critical scrutiny than it has so far received. Typically, in the essay quoted no account of what is meant by 'social justice' is offered. A commonsensical (in origin Aristotelian) understanding of justice is that it consists in the apportioning of reward or blame in accordance with what people merit or deserve. Let us assume that New

Labour's talk of justice presupposes this conception. Now, at the same time, New Labour is passionately committed to the maintenance and, where possible, extension of the market economy. This creates a major difficulty for their position (insofar as it aspires to coherence). For in a market economy the principle factors determining the distribution of material goods do not include merit or desert, or virtue or vice. ('Some rise by sin, and some by virtue fall.') This is empirically evident, and a phenomenon underlined by that high priest of marketism, Friedrich Hayek. As one recent summary of his thought states, 'those who come off better thanks to the operations of the market do not deserve their advantages... rather, they are luckier than their fellows...'

One of the reasons Aristotelian thinkers oppose capitalism is precisely that it is irremediably unjust, since, as well as apportioning advantages unjustly, its functioning involves the systematic manipulation of plain persons by politicians, advertisers, bureaucrats, managers et. al. As Stephen Knight puts it, in the introduction to *The MacIntyre Reader*:

> Capitalism is [...] a society which is structured by institutional manipulation of people in pursuit of goods of effectiveness [money, power and status]. Therefore, given the Aristotelian conception of justice as the virtue of treating people as they deserve, capitalism [...] is structurally unjust.

One cannot, that is to say, coherently be committed to both justice and capitalism. It is possible to accept the market economy and favour some degree of redistribution of wealth, which partially alleviates injustices in the distribution of goods. It is true that commitment to redistributive measures is often, if inaccurately, described as commitment to social justice. But since redistribution is not part of New Labour's project, it cannot be said to be in favour of social justice even in this loose sense.

The prospects of the Scottish economy in the context of globalising turbocapitalism are explored in an essay by Alf Young. His main point is that, if we are to succeed in the new world economic order, we must take to heart the philosophy of one Andy Grove, who, we learn, is CEO of Intel. This philosophy is summarised in the dictum 'only the paranoid survive.' Young suggests that this is not a thought congenial to most Scots, who are stuck in fuddy-duddy ways alien to the neo-capitalist culture which is emerging. However, failure to learn Grove's lesson will have the direst consequences: it is a message that 'each and every one of us ignores at his or her peril.' (Incidentally, the transformation of so many who only recently were leading figures of the Scottish left into devotees of US business ideology is a fascinating subject, which awaits proper investigation.)

Young is here voicing some of a set of assumptions which have become part of the conventional wisdom of many politicians, academics and columnists. These can be crudely expressed as follows. With the almost total collapse of oppositional ideas and structures, the world has been made safe for the investing and managing classes, and shall henceforth be administered in their interests, and as they deem fit. In such a world, driven above all by the ruthless pursuit of profit, only the most competitive can hope to survive. Competitiveness requires, among a range of other things, deregulation and a maximally flexibilised labour force, low levels of taxation, with a consequent reduction in welfare expenditure on non-productive sections of the population, investment in training for the frequent 're-skilling' of employees so that they can adapt to constant technological change, and the full exploitation of the opportunities offered by new technologies (such as, at present, the internet). Individuals, companies and countries unable or unwilling to participate in permanent capitalist revolution shall perish.

Some may well find this a hellish scenario, and consider that, far from preparing to be part of it, we ought urgently to be doing everything in our power to prevent it becoming reality. But it is really irrelevant whether we find it an attractive prospect or not. Nor is there any sense in asking whether the increased prosperity this future will bring us (or some of us, in some places) will make us happier or better people. For — a further assumption runs — this future is predestined, inevitable.

Such analyses invite several critical remarks. Firstly, the record of social prophecy is so poor that we have good reason to believe that, whatever the future will be like, it will bear little or no resemblance to the visions of present-day prophets. (Who in 1900 accurately predicted, or could have predicted, any of the major occurrences of the twentieth century?) Secondly, they are deeply deterministic, stating or implying that the majority of people are powerless, at the mercy of massive, irresistible and uncontrollable forces. This makes them intellectually suspect (consider the fate of Marxism, not as critique, but as another economistic theory of historical inevitability), and also ethically dubious, since they undermine people's belief that they can think and act to shape, to some extent at least, the kind of world they live in — and therefore also undermine their capacity to resist.

Rather ironically, the editors of *A Different Future* include in their introduction a quotation from Zygmunt Bauman's *In Search of Politics* which echoes some of these criticisms. Bauman is considering the paradox that, although free societies have triumphed over totalitarianisms, people feel powerless. Our freedom is not felt to include the freedom to conceive and effect a different kind of future:

> If freedom has won, how does it come about that human ability to imagine a better world and to do something about that human ability to imagine a better world and to do something to make it better was not among the trophies of victory? And what kind of freedom is it that discourages imagination and tolerates the impotence of free people in matters that concern them?

In the contributions on education, it is acknowledged that the educational system faces serious problems: there is conflict between policy-makers and practitioners, and many young people leave school without skills or qualifications. But no sense is conveyed of the real crisis which exists, or of how dire the situation is in some areas of education and training. Schoolteachers are overstretched and demoralised. If education really were the political priority it is constantly declared to be, measures would be being taken, for instance, to ensure that teachers enjoyed the same kind of status and recognition as they do in countries like France or Germany. Such steps are not on political agenda, so we will continue to have a third-rate and declining state-school system. Its performance is dismal, despite the official jargon about commitment to 'excellence,' the denials that standards are falling, and the apparent self-satisfaction of the educational establishment. (To choose one sorry instance from many, in 1997 an international survey of achievement in mathematics and science among thirteen-year-olds placed Scotland 26th and 29th respectively, out of 41 countries; in each case it came behind even England.)

To turn to theoretical issues. What is the relationship between educational and other social activities? And — a related question — what is the point of education?

It is difficult to identify any clear responses to such basic questions in present-day discussion about education, in much of which theorising about education is confused with demonstrating allegiance to bland slogans like 'lifelong learning,' familiarity with a host of abbreviations and acronyms, and an ability to use terms borrowed from the ghastly lexis of managerialism. (Public discourse in general is now largely a matter of shuffling around a set of standard expressions: embarrassing cliches like 'addressing the issue' and 'getting the balance right,' together with such words as 'empowerment,' 'pro-active,' 'step-change,' 'stakeholding,' and other important-sounding mumbo-jumbo. The use of this poverty-stricken language, which severely constricts thought and makes it impossible to discuss anything of importance, is clearly itself a modality of power.)

One contributor writes: 'The emerging shape of the world in which [today's children] will live and work, calls for visionary and ambitious educational responses.' Another states that 'there is much to be said for a demand-led approach to determining priorities.' What these comments suggest is that education is essentially a subordinate practice, whose role it is to serve (respond to and be led by) independently evolving social processes and practices; and also that educational and other activities function in harmony. An alternative view is that education can and should help shape the social whole; that it is part of the educator's task to encourage questioning and criticism of society; and that, as the philosopher John Anderson emphasised, education is a 'separate interest,' which requires intransigent defence against the encroachment of state, business and other non-educational interests.

Today such encroachment is massive, and growing. In most educational discussion, although lip-service may be paid to such vague goals as 'personal development,' it is assumed that the primary purpose of education is to provide preparation and training for employment; and resources are being increasingly directed to IT, business studies, and other vocational subjects.

In these circumstances, the tradition of democratic intellectualism (or education as an introduction to culture for all) would seem to be something of a lost cause. Be that as it may, the humanist conception of education as being principally concerned with culture and criticism, defended by Anderson and George Davie, has recently been restated by one of the world's foremost philosophers. Everyone, says Alasdair MacIntyre, needs to study history, mathematics, physics, astronomy, literature, classical Greek, a modern foreign language, music and art; moreover, courses in philosophy should be compulsory for undergraduates. Echoing the point made by Anderson that failure to develop understanding means developing submissiveness, MacIntyre sees one of the purposes of this type of education as the formation of resistance to manipulation.

It will be objected that such an education is not a suitable preparation for success in a society like ours. MacIntyre fully agrees that this proposition is true. What he disputes is the idea that it amounts to an objection:

> Of course an education of this kind would require a major shift in our resources and priorities, and, if successful, it would produce in our students habits of mind which unfit them for the contemporary world. But to unfit our students for the contemporary world ought in any case to be one of our educational aims.

A debate which also engaged with counter-systemic positions such as MacIntyre's would permit and encourage what conventional political discussion excludes: argument over first principles, and the examination of all assumptions. It is really only a debate of this kind that can allow us to raise the fundamental questions we most need to ask and attempt to answer.

In a deeply conformist age, a heavy responsibility rests on academics and intellectuals to develop and disseminate critical ideas, and to draw attention to ways of seeing the world which do not accord with the now dominant, normally unquestioned perspectives, and to do these things in ways which reach beyond purely academic and elite audiences. (To avoid a possible misunderstanding: this is a call for social dialogue, not intellectual vanguardism. It is arguable that, for instance, among the poor and sub-poor there is in fact today a much clearer and more critical understanding of political and social realities than exists in academic and intellectual circles.) The churches, too, have an important role to perform, in defence of the values and traditions of thought they represent, or ought to represent — values and traditions which, if taken seriously, can only be sources of theoretical and practical opposition and resistance to current dispensations.

Ronald Turnbull is co-author, with Craig Beveridge, of *The Eclipse of Scottish Culture* and *Scotland after Enlightenment*.

Reviews

Slavoj Zizek — Naomi Klein — Modern Catalan Plays — David Greig — Lluisa Cunillé — Miles Glendinning & David Page — Neil Davidson — H.V. Morton — redefining progress — Duncan Glen — Tony Lopez

Edinburgh Review seeks to publish an eclectic selection of reviews covering small small press material, books of Scottish interest and works of contemporary philosophical, political and cultural thought. Please send books for review for the attention of the Reviews Editor, Edinburgh Review, 22a Buccleuch Place, Edinburgh, EH8 9LN

Slavoj Zizek — *The Ticklish Subject:*
the absent centre of political ontology
Verso pbk £15.00
ISBN 1 85984 894 X

Benjamin Arditi & Jeremy Valentine —
Polemicization: The Contingency of the
Commonplace
Edinburgh University Press pbk £16.95
ISBN 0 7486 1064 2

Naomi Klein — *No Logo*
Flamingo pbk £14.99
ISBN 0 00 255919 6

THE DISRUPTION of the human sciences that
was registered first in literary studies has
been slowly spreading. The eruption
of what were once dismissed as post-
structuralism has also begun to make its
mark on political theory and cultural
studies as well as in some departments of
(mostly continental) philosophy. Literary
studies happily settled down into a de-
politicised historicism. But the eruption of
this foreign body into political thought has
been at the level of rethinking the political
itself.

The first two of these books, Zizek's and
Arditi and Valentine's, might be said to
participate in this translation, each in their
own ways, while the interest of Naomi
Klein's book is that she is unable to do so.
This translation is that of both the
evolution of the object of political theory
from politics as empirical practice to the
concept of politics itself (and may be seen
as a response, at least in part, to the
disappearance of easily demarcated left and
right politics), and a translation of thought
from one language to another. The

difficulty Zizek, Arditi and Valentine fact
is that their respective books must act as
both messenger (even if what they carry
may turn out to be contagious, infectious
— some French disease), and interpreter.
The results are by turn fascinating and
frustrating.

Slavoj Zizek's latest work for Verso
attempts to defend a conception of
Cartesian subjectivity against what he sees
as three key onslaughts: in the heritage of
German Idealism (from Heidegger to
Habermas); in post-Althusserian political
philosophy (Alan Badiou in particular);
and in Anglo-American leftist and
deconstructionist cultural studies (his
example here is Judith Butler). Sadly for
those traditionalists looking for a final
putting to rest of all such postmodern
nonsense, Zizek does all this in the name
of a subject defined rather more by Lacan
than by Aristotle.

Nevertheless, it's a dazzling procession,
in which the author skips from language to
language, thinker to thinker, theory to
example, high culture to low. It's all
performed somewhat in the manner of a
universal translating machine, in which
Judith Butler and Julia Roberts, Hegel and
the X-Files are thrown into relation. This is
what Zizek is famous for, of course, and
what makes him so readable. Although, as
with that other island of discursive clarity
in the murky waters of theory, Terry
Eagleton, I begin to suspect that something is being carefully, and decisively, put
aside to achieve this.

Ultimately of course, for Zizek, all
cultural currencies are convertible into
Lacan, which is rather the problem as far
as I'm concerned. But even for someone

who is open to agreement with Zizek, his style of argument will remain problematic — as I said, it's a dazzling procession, in which the rapidity of the switches between subjects and the brevity of the discussions are precisely arranged to suit the author's own purposes rather than to develop an rounded account of the texts he discusses.

This is particularly noticeable in Zizek's first section which runs from Hegel to Kant (via Heidegger and Derrida). Elsewhere his discussion of Badiou is illuminating, though does not engage the other thinkers he challenges — Laclau, Ranciere and Balibar — as successfully as Zizek would like.

Strangely, *The Ticklish Subject* is most convincing when Zizek is not hiding behind erudition — for example in his call to repoliticise that which is taken as the inevitable ground of politics and therefore seen as beyond politics: the economic. This is not intended to replace the politics of identity, or single issue campaigns, but to provide a ground for them both — though what Zizek means by this is not clear.

Zizek remains resolutely optimistic, an unusual tone in contemporary continental political thought, and has a charming faith in the ultimate demise of the capitalist system he attempts to analyse: 'the very inherent antagonism of a system may well set in motion a process which leads to its own ultimate demise'. If you believe that the today's subject can be characterised as proto-paranoiac, maybe they'll be something for you in *The Ticklish Subject* — if not, you will at least find some pertinent questions addressed to theorists who more often inspire discipleship than analysis (Deleuze for example).

Zizek might also be a suitable antidote to the liberal hand-wringing of Naomi Klein's *No Logo*. Klein is a Canadian journalist and her book walks the uneasy line that those in the media who seek to criticise their own position must tread. A refreshingly easily read after Zizek's Lacanian psycho-babble, this is a simplistic account of the conflicts between the marketing of global capitalism and the young activists who are trying to articulate their opposition to that system. The problem is the speed with which the contemporary advertising industry can adopt and neutralise any oppositional position as a new marketing strategy: alternative cool.

Behind a certain amount of brow-beating about multinational corporations, Klein documents some interesting forms of resistance. However, rather than prescribing a revolutionary approach to capital as such, she seems to suggest that a paliative or ameliorative change just is taking place, and mainly in the media.

For Klein, the symbolic contestation of capital by the rag-tag alliances of Christian, Union and anarchist groups mobilising against third world debt or trading double standrards doesn't simply serve an affirmative function, but a liberatory one. Her inability to theorise her position reduces this to cappucino-leftist neo-yuppie whining.

Klein's account of culture-jamming — symbolic violence directed at subverting or exposing the big blobal brands — is telling. Often the jammers work for advertising companies themselves, using the tools of their trade to produce what really only amount to glossy parodies.

Which might go down as an example of polemicization in Arditi and Valentine's terms. Their book recasts the rethinking of the political, terms of the persistence of antagonism in the public sphere. Polemicization attempts to name the moment at which oppositional and polemical engagements fail; revealing that they are predicated on a gap between symbolic and real order. This in turn throws the place of enunciation, the social space — the place of being in common — into disorder, or at least opens it to questioning.

Polemicization is thought-provoking, but distracting on account not only of its own polemical rhetoric but also because of its attempt to coalesce and coerce a wide range of distinct theoretical positions in support of its argument. The authors veer alarmingly from Kant to deconstruction, Chantal Mouffe to Michel Foucault, as if these were merely building blocks rather than complex theoretical positions in themselves. Where Zizek attempts to sum up the whole work of his opponents in a few lines, Arditi and Valentine quote short extracts with little attempt at contextualisation. Thus a writer like Derrida can be co-opted to a position he would never take himself.

Like Zizek, Valentine and Arditi have a master-thinker in whose work they draw at length. In their case, it is Jacques Ranciere, whose distinction between 'police' and 'political,' which invokes an authentic and disruptive moment of politicisation to disrupt the political philosophies and sociological attempts to put an end to politics, underlies much of *Polemicization*. In turn this is open to the charge put by

Zizek to Ranciere, that the political as the marginalised force (against the police) depends on the impossibility of its success, of actually changing the relationship within which it is defined. As in Zizek's account of Badiou's truth events (an unexpected event which betrays the fundamental political logic of its time) which appear decidedly messianic, or divinely-inspired, there is little room left for agency in Valentine and Arditi's account.

Both *The Ticklish Subject* and *Polemicization* are worthy of careful consideration; but they will not do as introductions to the scene of translation I sketched out at the beginning of this review. Instead they are more akin to *inductions*, foregrounding rather than dismantling the hermeticism of such debates. In fact, readers should be wary of the persuasive ease with which everything is put into question so quickly, so little discussed and so much concluded. Mind you, a little time with their notes and bibliographies would yield a fascinating reading list.

There is a constant temptation to pathos in political theory — to raise the stakes with grievous empirical injustices which no mere book will atone for; but also to take urgency as an excuse to hurry reflection. These books seem to me to partake in this economy of haste. I wonder whether there might not be an alternative — but neither a fashionable, nor a comfortable one — approach? In which case, as far as I'm concerned, the question to answer mght be how to rearticulate *patience* (taken to mean not only *waiting* but, in its original form, *suffering*) with political practice.

John Seabrook – *Nobrow: The Culture of Marketing; The Marketing of Culture*
Methuen pbk £9.99
ISBN 0 413 74470 1

John Seabrook's *Nobrow* is a chronicle of the commercialisation of American culture told through the author's association with *The New Yorker* magazine, where under Tina Brown's editorship he was assigned to subjects such as MTV, George Lucas's 'Skywalker Ranch', and media-mogul David Geffen. These profiles, and many others, provide Seabrook with illustration and inspiration for his contention that we are at what he calls the 'Nobrow' position, 'the exact midpoint at which culture and marketing converge.'

Seabrook argues that we have witnessed the death of 'townhouse' culture. The high-cultural artist claimed to produce their work according to spontaneous intuitions, without regard for the capital risk involved in the reproduction and distribution of their product. Mass culture, however, uses market research to forecast as accurately as it can the potential demand for the latest product in order to make the capital investment as safe as possible. The twentieth century, though, has seen a gradual closing of the circuit between art and economy; all artists are now inheritors of a commercially informed tradition.

Nobrow culture offers, so Seabrook claims, an illusion of resistance to this process by promising contact with the spontaneity which was once supplied by appreciation of the work of a genius. Now, instead of Wordsworth and Beethoven, brands such as Porn Star and Yellow Rat Bastard gesture towards a grass-roots that has sprung up between the paving stones of commercial culture. The subcultures of skateboarders and urban gangs can be appropriated by the appropriate logo; but this magical identification can only last briefly before these cultural markers are swallowed up by what Seabrook refers to as the 'big-grid' of corporate production. (In the United Kingdom, we might think of the fate of urban camouflage patterns. These originally appeared in the early nineties in street fashions based around military surplus, and were subsequently worn by girl bands who publicised them to the nation. By the end of the decade, urban camouflage trousers and jackets were available in Marks and Spencers, in children's sizes.)

An individual, in the Nobrow world, is therefore not defined by autonomous action, but by a collection of brand affiliations which carry an aura of authenticity – like 'a snowboarder who listens to classical music, drinks Coke, and loves Quentin Tarantino' or 'a World Cup soccer fan who wears FUBU and likes opera.' The individual is differentiated, but only in obedience to the demands of capital for investment in new markets.

Perhaps the biggest fault with *Nobrow* is Seabrook's ambivalence about the status of this Nobrow self. Is there anything more to one's uniqueness than obedience to an ultimately capitalist demand that one should be different? Or can human difference be more (or less) authentic and spontaneous – 'from the heart', so to speak? *Nobrow* is dogged by a sense of nostalgia for the 'genius' of the artist, but, at the same time, Seabrook has little truck with what, he claims, 'was always in part a clever marketing exercise.' This obscurity is also related to the other big problem with *Nobrow*: Seabrook allows himself to be bogged down by endless gossipy illustrations of his thesis – so much so, that it's hard to make out what he's actually arguing.

Despite these problems, *Nobrow* is a readable, interesting and useful addition to a debate which is too often couched in lofty abstractions and cryptic mottoes. Anyone who wants to know what the 'culture industry' looks like today could find much worse places to start than Seabrook's accessible and well-exemplified writing.

John London & David George eds. —
Modern Catalan Plays
Methuen pbk £10.99
ISBN 0 413 74440 X

David Greig — *The Speculator*
Lluïsa Cunillé — *The Meeting*
both trans. John London
Methuen pbk £7.99
ISBN 0 413 74310 1

COMMENTATORS HAVE, particularly since devolution, been keen to draw parallels between Scotland and Catalonia. And who can blame them: in many respects it is the Catalan example of autonomy, national pride and wealth, within a larger state, that sets the target for Scottish devolutionary ambitions. Scotland aims to recreate Catalonia's prosperity, the buzz and creativity of its main cities and the confidence of its cultural identity. Unfortunately, judging by the ongoing whinging over the new Parliament

building, Barcelona's architectural brilliance certainly looks beyond Scottish ambition.

In this collection of modern Catalan plays, all first performed in the 1990s, John London rightly points out that nobody would have paid the slightest attention to the theatre of Catalonia until the last decade and a half. To a certain extent Catalan theatre has made itself known to the outside world on the coat-tails of other arts forms, particularly architecture and design; after all it does face the particular problem of existing in a minority Romance language not immediately accessible to the rest of Europe. It is in the language, however, that one of the strengths of Catalan theatre, and unfortunate weakness of these translations, appears.

Through-out the period of Franco's rule Catalan culture, and its language in particular, were actively suppressed. In this context theatre became a powerful, but also mobile and intangible, public expression of identity and of language. Theatre can disappear and evade official detection more easily than written texts. Rodolf Sirera, one of the playwrights in this collection, declared theatre 'a political weapon' with which to fight Franco. This linguistic strength and heritage is, however, almost impossible for the outsider to access. Often the political nature of the plays is imbedded in their being performed in Catalan, something which is inevitably lost when they are translated into English. Translation into Scots isn't an adequate solution, while most Catalans are bilingual; most Scots are not.

This difference in attitudes to language

begins to hint at the far larger cultural differences between Scotland and Catalonia, and how these two nations view their larger neighbours, than the easy parallel of their respective hopes for devolution. This aspect clearly emerged when a new Scottish and a new Catalan play were commissioned alongside each other for the 1999 Edinburgh International Festival. David Greig's *The Speculator* and Lluïsa Cunillé's *The Meeting* appeared in Barcelona in Catalan, and then in Edinburgh in English, and both are now published together by Methuen as 'two plays about cultural identity.'

Perhaps inevitably the plays have virtually nothing in common. Greig's play is a baroque, ambitious and sprawling tale of John Law, a Scot in Paris, inventor of paper money and for a brief period the richest man in the world. If *The Speculator* is about cultural identity then it is locked within the familiar theme of the Scots inventor, explorer or soldier, the wee man in the world, a theme which is far less interesting than the play's other questions regarding wealth, money, value and price. Cunillé's play on the other hand is stark, apparently much more limited in its ambition and short, with, I expect, any exploration of national identity locked up within the language.

Intriguingly three of the four plays in the collection *Modern Catalan Plays* share an immediate and peculiar element with *The Meeting*: from this brief survey it appears that Catalan playwrights are not in the habit of giving characters' names. Instead they are populated by The Female Watchmaker, The Doctor, Old Man, Daughter, First Old Woman, Second Old

Woman, and even Man, Woman and She. This anonymity fits the barrenness of all of these plays; and also their language, which in translation is also stark and bare, sounding almost proverbial. A typical exchange from the first play in the collection, Joan Brossa's *The Quarrelsome Party*:

OLD WOMAN: He who knows names
    should know that there are things that
    can't be named.
OLD MAN: Why are you telling me this?
OLD WOMAN: Because before being weak
    you have to be strong.
OLD MAN: Thinking about it, you're right.
OLD WOMAN: Of course, you mortal man.

It is interesting to wonder how this could be performed, as it is neither naturalistic nor stylised in a familiar (perhaps Pinteresque) fashion. During the International Festival *The Meeting* was performed slowly and seriously, but perhaps there are odd and peculiar laughs in these plays — underneath the surface of the words. This is certainly the case in the second act of Brossa's play where an extended dialogue between three elderly characters is interrupted regularly as each in turn excuses themselves and leaves the stage for a couple of minutes, happening again and again and again. These regular exits imitate and then parody the rituals of drawing room farce, provide the characters with innumerable opportunities to talk behind each others' backs, yet they are also rooted in the realness and banality of weak bladders.

Two other plays in the collection share this habit of anonymous character titles.

Josep Maria Benet i Jornet's *Desire* perhaps also exists within a proverbial, fabelistic, landscape, but one which is twisted by the addition of a contemporarily menacing atmosphere. Through-out the play something always seems to be on the verge of happening (a chisel makes numerous appearances, cars are parked on the side of empty country roads, characters lie, evade, and contradict themselves) yet never does. John London introduces the play by making references to two films: first, to Hitchcock which I can see in the tension and apprehension that the play seeks to create; second, to *Basic Instinct* a parallel which left me more than a little baffled.

Sergi Belbel's *Fourplay* (featuring The Woman, The Man, The Male Friend and The Female Friend) is a superb dramatic exercise in time, place and action. Thirty eight short scenes are played out in a single windowless room containing only a small bed, the plot involving a series of sometimes farcical, sometimes erotic, encounters between the four characters in the room and across the bed.

And there is a plot, but one which Belbel has cut up and rearrange so that each odd-numbered scene takes the story back in time while each even-numbered scene moves the narrative forwards — exactly in the middle of the play the plot carried in these two directions meets and the whole thing is played out again in reverse this time with slightly different spin upon each scene. (A strip tease appears confident and erotic the first time around; seen a second time, when we know more about the character, it is clumsy and sad.) Slowly the reader pieces together the scenes until a complete picture is constructed, yet the slight twists in the second half the question how certain this understanding is and ask us to consider how we respond to what we see and how we make judgements. On the page it is simply there, coolly intellectual; performed fast on the stage it could work fantastically.

Finally, there is the one play in the collection where the character's have names, Rodolf Sirera's *The Audition*. Set in Paris in 1784 Sirera's is in part a trick, with the audience kept in the dark about a serious of plot twists. In part it is philosophical, examining Diderot's discussion of the different persuasive power of an actor who draws on genuine feeling and one who is more self-controlled. Here this question is asked regarding the stage performance of death — can an actor who is not actually dying (and who cannot know what it would be like to die) 'die' convincingly? Or is the only option to stage tragic drama as snuff plays where, in an absolute example of live performance, the actor dies with his character? I can't say much more, as to do so would give away the twists.

**Miles Glendinning and David Page —
*Clone City, Crisis and Renewal in
Contemporary Scottish Architecture*
Polygon pbk £11.99
ISBN 0 7486 6255 3**

This is an ambitious book. It calls on all of us to reclaim architecture for democracy — to reflect upon and control the cities we inhabit — instead of simply 'accepting what is handed to us.' The title is one of the most arresting metaphors. 'Clone City' refers to the mind-boggling diversity of suburban neighbourhoods popping up around Scotland's central belt which, though all different and individually branded, nonetheless look the same. This is urban development which lacks any coherence (developments can appear anywhere) but which is, at the same time, characterised by commodified homogenisation. The book is a powerful attack on the mindless market-driven proliferation of 'separate brick boxes' which is the reality of (sub-)urban development in Scotland today.

The authors, an architectural historian and an architect respectively, are masters of the broad stroke. They summarise the history of Scottish architecture in a few engaging pages. But they are also acutely aware of the importance of detail; they supply superbly researched examples to back up their case when appropriate. Beautiful aerial pictures are used to good effect. Though sometimes dated, they are so stunning that they make the book worth having even if you have no intention of reading it.

That said, *Clone City* leaves a lot to be desired. Its prose is hyperbolic and difficult to penetrate. It is highly readable, but for experts only. For a book that attempts to initiate a democratic debate on Scottish architecture (which goes beyond the endless arguments surrounding the building of the Scottish parliament itself) its language is simply inappropriate. Terms such as 'Fordism,' 'Taylorism,' 'Functionalism' or even 'progress' litter the argument with little explanation. Some terms, such as 'capitalism,' are used very vaguely; some, like 'postmodernism,' are defined in a manner which would not make sense to anyone unfamiliar with the canon of writing on postmodern architecture.

The erudite attack on the 'Clone City' is the real strength of this book — in contrast, the solutions the authors advance are often rather disappointing. The problem isn't that the alternatives offered fail to make sense: there clearly is a need for more effective regional planning in Scotland (especially after local government reorganisation in 1996 abolished regional councils); there is a case for considering the Central Belt as one big urban mass — as Patrick Geddes's 'Clydeforth'; the authors' call to rethink and, at times, move the Green Belt is, while controversial, certainly coherent. But while the plea to actively embrace planning for Clydeforth in order to fight urban fragmentation is worthy of debate, the idea to develop New Towns to absorb excess populations is old-hat, however, and has for England at least, been challenged more forcefully by Sir Peter Hall and Colin Ward in their seminal *Sociable Cities* (Wiley, London 1998)

But there's a more fundamental paradox in this book. After attacking 'Clone City' urban sprawl, the authors still urge us to accept and even embrace suburban development. They praise car-dependent and aesthetically disastrous edge-of-town development such as Edinburgh Park (which David Page had a hand in as an architect). Meanwhile, their call for more public transport is welcome, but at the same time a naive commonplace. Better public transport alone will not deliver more desirable and sustainable neighbourhoods (just look at Paris). The history of planning is littered with visionaries such as Geddes or Howard (whom the authors cite approvingly) demanding public-transport based New Towns and, in practice, achieving car-dependent East Kilbrides. What reason do Glendinning and Page have, one wonders, to assume that their New Town proposals will fare any better in the harsh market-driven world which they themselves describe?

Despite its shortcomings, however, this book has to be welcomed in its boldness. If it manages to rekindle a debate on Scottish urban life; if it helps us to realise that cities are not places we merely inhabit, but places we must collectively shape, this books deserves our unqualified praise.

Neil Davidson — *The Origins of Scottish Nationhood*
Pluto pbk £14.99
ISBN 0 7453 1608

H.V.Morton — *In Search of Scotland*
Methuen pbk £8.99
ISBN 0 413 54480 X

THESE TWO books are both concerned with the myths of Scotland; but where Morton's 1920s travel narrative is concerned to confirm and disseminate them, Davidson sets out to demolish them. Read together, they make an interesting case study in the historiography of Scotland.

Morton's book has value only as a curiosity — a naïve period piece. An account of the author's first visit to Scotland, it was first developed as a series of newspaper articles. It's a relic from another age, one in which Englishmen were real Englishmen, and Scotsmen were everything expected of them by the urbane cosmopolitan observer.

What is most revealing is that Morton

already knows Scotland, has internalised its myths, without ever having stepped across the border. Here's a sample, just for fun: 'I am all alone at the Border, one foot in England, the other in Scotland. There is a metal post with 'Scotland' written on it. It is a superfluous post. You do not need to be told that you have come to the end of England. Carter Bar is indeed a gate: the historic barrier between Celt and Saxon.'

All nonsense of course. What Morton thinks he recognises is an invention; the Scots' country is Scott country. The history of Scotland is first and foremost the effort to disentangle the myths of Scotland. The most recent mutation in this is the advent of more sophisticated ways of dealing with myth than either affirming them, or smashing them.

Neil Davidson's *The Origins of Scottish Nationhood* is an attempt to do just this. rather than simply to deny the myth and replace it with another 'reality', he instead tries to set the mythification of Scotland into its own historical context, focusing particularly on the century or so after Union. Doing so makes 'Scotland' look like a distinctly dubious proposition, and Davidson insists that Scottish national identity cannot be examined in distinction from three other key factors.

Firstly, Scottish nationhood is inseparable from Britishness; it is also an Imperial construct, and Davidson rejects any assertion (the example is David Macrone's) that Scotland was a 'junior partner' in the British empire; and thirdly, it Scottish identity only comes into being once the mythology and imagery of the Highlands have been absorbed by the

Lowlands. Davidson insists that the divisions between Lowland and Highland render any discussion of a Scotland pre-Union meaningless, and that the atrocities of the Clearances should be blamed on the Lowlands officers, not on the English.

All this demystification enables Davidson to take a traditional Marxist line against nationalism, arguing that nations are mythic (an older vocabulary would call them ideological) constructions, designed to mask the reality of life for Scotland's population — and that the idea of the 'Scottish people' is itself a veil for the reality of class-divided Scotland.

However Davidson's analysis of the class structure of Scotland at the time seems flimsy when compared with the empirical and documentary evidence on which the earlier discussion has been based. His chapter on Scott and Burns in particular, which only seems to serve to warn us that their positions are both complex and ambiguous, is slight compared with what has preceded it.

Naturally, the real aims of Davidson's book lie not in the past, but in the present. By undermining the naturalised idea of Scottish nationhood, he hopes to expose the political basis of these myths. This is a valuable project, but it meets its own limits once the myths have been described, and their origins traced, for it doesn't necessarily suggest one political outcome now. Unless, of course, we reinstate the old distinction between myth and reality. If we're simply constructing myths, why should a nationalist one be worse than a socialist one?

In an interesting 'Afterword' Davidson defends himself against nationalist approaches which have acknowledged that the idea of nation is indeed mythical, but that there is nothing to replace it, and that nations just happen to be the space of political engagement. As Davidson correctly observes, these accounts have to assume that the nation is itself a natural formation, or to some extent, that nations just *are*.

Yet Davidson is unable to oppose anything to the nationalist myth except his own myth, which is, unsurprisingly, that of a Scottish working class. Which would leave his own work open to attack in a work of precisely the same type as his own. Both positions are forms of historicism: an idealisation of a existing structure which predicts it into the future. Davidson imagines a future without nations. Yet mightn't we do better to begin from the problem of identity itself, and ask why we should have to make a choice at all?

Davidson wonders whether the politics of nationalism can ever escape being (implicitly at least) based on a principle of the exclusion of those who do not belong, and while this is an important issue he never comes to terms with the ways it might equally be applied to his own politics. What are the limits of Marxism? Where are the boundaries of the working class? Yet this book is far more than a piece of polemic; and its clear and comprehensive account of the debate is useful even when at times, enthusiasm leads its author astray.

How far have we come then, from T.V. Morton's literary tourism? Perhaps only to the limits of myth, but not beyond.

Redefining Progress
www.rprogress.org

IT IS OFTEN difficult for environmental campaigners and think tanks to convey to politicians and policy makers, and to the public in general, the 'big picture' of global sustainability. We are not only much more interested in, but are also simply much more able to comprehend, our own backyard; it is not easy, nor instinctive, to think on a wider, a macro, a global scale.

This simple problem is one which Redefining Progress, a San Francisco based think tank with an extremely useful web presence, faces. It is also a problem which they begin to address with a neat little interactive internet gimmick — a simple questionnaire which the average surfer can fill in and use to quickly calculate their ecological footprint. An ecological footprint is your personal impact on the Earth: the amount of land and water you occupy to produce all the resources you consume and to take in all the waste you produce — measured in terms of surface area.

The average America has an ecological footprint of 25 acres, roughly 25 football pitches; the average Canadian exists on 25% less and the average Italian on over 60% less than this American benchmark. The actual space available for each person in the world, if things were shared out equally and none was reserved for anything except humans, is 5.5 acres. These figures, however, mean little until you get to do the calculations for yourself, which is what the ecological footprint calculator allows you to do: filling in general details regarding your lifestyle from the size of

your house, to the food you eat and the number of miles you travel by car a year.

The programme, which you can access either through Redefining Progress's site or via a slightly more user friendly and metric version at www.mec.ca, then calculates your own personal ecological footprint and indicates how many planets would be needed to allow everybody in the world to enjoy your standard of living. Personally, I make do on 7.93 acres, 31.5% of the American average, but still almost double the global mean. Clearly feeling that everybody has a right to something like the standard of living that I enjoy, and that I would not willingly cut back my lifestyle too desperately, I tried to fiddle the figures but still could not fit everybody onto one Earth. Adding in room for other life forms (the Rio summit suggests a measly 12%) and I still needed more than twice as much room then is currently available.

No wonder that the footprint calculator is introduced with a warning: 'The results your answers produce may disturb you. In a few reported cases the users' well-being was affected and some serious thinking was induced.' This is a simple little game to play, it takes only a few minutes, yet is also one of the most powerful illustration I have come across of the real, global, environmental blind alley that we as a global population seem to be taking.

It is these questions that Redefining Progress is attempting to tackle, as a quick trawl of the rest of their site demonstrates. They seek, in short, to correct the imbalance in what Oscar Wilde famously described as the difference between knowing the price of everything and the value of nothing. How can a culture which prices everything according to the market, that measures progress by GDP, account for none market benefits such as safe streets, clean air, and biodiversity? Answers might take up slightly more room than a postcard.

Julian Goodare and Michael Lynch (eds.) — *The Reign of James VI* Tuckwell pbk £16.99 ISBN 1 86232 095 0

IT IS REMARKABLE that the Scottish reign of King James VI has been so little studied, when there is now considerable scholarly and even popular interest in the years which saw major debates over Presbyterianism, the great renewal of Scots court poetry and the Union of the Crowns. *The Reign of James VI* is an important collection of essays and some of the best new writing on early modern Scotland is on display here, which makes the diffident tone of some of the introductory passages seem a little misplaced. Goodare and Lynch's leading essay is punctuated by pessimistic references to 'black holes in our knowledge' and 'an erratic, bewildering process of change'. Yet the evidence of this book itself suggests that modern research is beginning to describe, coherently and in detail, the complex events of this period.

A great strength of the volume is the way in which the individual essays are clearly focused on particular areas, yet always aware of broader contexts. Care is taken to set James's reign in the context of the medieval and early sixteenth-century past, and several writers have no hesitation in looking forward to the conflicts of the mid-seventeenth century. Julian Goodare

suggests that James 'left his son a malign legacy,' which should provoke a response from other 'revisionist' writers who see the Civil War as a wholly unexpected disruption. Equally, Ruth Grant's essay describes particular incidents in Scottish politics within the frame of political and religious conflicts in Counter-Reformation Western Europe as a whole.

Praise must also go to the essays dealing with subjects which tend to be glossed over in more general histories of Scotland or Britain; it will no longer be possible to allude casually to James's dependence on an English subsidy, or the colonising attitude of the Edinburgh government towards the Borders and Highlands. There is a wealth of new theoretical approaches and clearly presented factual information in the essays by Goodare, Lynch and Sharon Adams, which lay the basis for much future scholarship. Several essays do an excellent job of trying to get at the truth behind post-Jacobean agglomerations of myth and rumour, none more so than Alan MacDonald's sharp analysis of the complex situation in the Kirk, which has been over-simplified by using traditional terminology such as 'the Black Acts' and 'the Golden Acts'.

Several essays could benefit from a little more space, in order to treat their subject on the same scale as other areas. Grant Simpson's important 'short commentary' on James's neglected personal letters includes a couple of valuable annotated texts, but it would have been good to see some discussion of the later correspondence, which Simpson dismisses as 'poor stuff', although the letters to Buckingham and his family offer remarkable insights into James's ever-changing attitudes to gender and sexuality. Again, Maureen Meikle makes an interesting case for a reconsideration of Queen Anna as an active political figure, but it would be really useful to know more about her motives for supporting the unpredictable Earl of Bothwell, and the circumstances of her conversion to Catholicism (although there seems to be an understandable shortage of evidence regarding the latter).

It is good to see that this volume breaks new ground in including writing on the culture, literature and architecture of Jacobean Scotland, along with more traditionally historical essays. I found the material in Aonghus MacKechnie's essay both new and particularly fascinating. On the other hand I would like to see the assertion made by both Julian Goodare and Jenny Wormald, that James wrote his first Biblical commentary in 1588, qualified by a reference to the fact that the editor of James's 1617 *Workes* identifies the intriguing *Paraphrase Upon the Revelation*, first printed in that volume, as having been composed in the early 1580s.

More tentatively, I would also question the tendency of several writers to denigrate the quality of James's later writings. Rod Lyall's excellent essay on James's position in the 'Castalian' poetic revival makes the claim that James's poetic gifts were drying up by 1588 (what about the sonnets introducing *Basilicon Doron*, or the political satires of the 1620s?) Jenny Wormald dismisses the *Meditation on St. Matthew* (1620) as the dull product of a sad decline, although its outrageous attempt to compare the burden of kingship to the suffering of Christ clearly influenced

Charles I's attitude to royal martyrdom. James's style and literary technique certainly changed, not least because of the increasing Anglicisation of his language, but there is perhaps a need for a revisionist reappreciation of the later works, although it might not, admittedly, find a place in a collection focused on Scotland.

Jenny Wormald's essay should whet the appetites of those who have been looking forward to her new biography of James. Her controversial but compelling analysis of James's experience of culture and politics in England after 1603, and the ways in which a highly successful Scottish king was overwhelmed by the chaos of English politics and rhetoric, shows that there is still much room for new writing about James's self-presentation in his writings. We must hope that the appearance of that book will in its turn stimulate much more interdisciplinary work on James.

Raymond Friel & Richard Price — *Renfrewshire in Old Photographs* Mariscat Press pbk £6.00 ISBN 0 946588 21 X

(Mariscat Press, 3 Mariscat Road, Glasgow G41 4ND)

Despite its title, this volume is a collection of poetry by the two authors, with half of the book given to each. The title alludes to the creative process involved — both poets have employed photographic local histories as inspiration.

Friel works, it appears, from a specific book of images, *Greenock from Old Photographs*. 'Wee Dublin' shows a Greenock haunted by the conversation of ancestral spirits. In the punning 'crack of flames,' there are 'ghosts who spoke/ another, lighter language' – a language distinct from that heard in the Catholic 'chanting pilgrimage/ to the teeming slopes/ of Paradise.' With their 'free-wheeling fiddles,' these spirits have cheated the profit-and-loss calculations demanded by the Christian afterlife.

Price's sequence continues this disillusionment with narratives of redemption. The conceit of 'Hillman Avenger' is a new crucifixion – with the eponymous, Linwood-built car as the cross, and Barochan Hill as Golgotha. This is a cross with a small 'c', however, because Renfrewshire is not a place where divine (or state) intervention can work. In 'Reservoir', the speaker informs us that 'there are no miracles/ on a Council loch, By ORDER'

A playful neo-paganism therefore replaces submission to a thundering patriarch (whether divine or political). In 'Dry Bed', returning life is heralded during the Winter Solstice as 'On the shortest day the woolly sun/ drives the family crate,/ holed lamps light the coupé:/ re-engined bright.' A trick of the light, a pleasing illusion, offers resurrection through the 'woolly sun', an entity quite distinct from the sacrificial Lamb provided by the Son of God. Renfrewshire is, Price would say, 'a small place.' Its value is precisely in its testimony to a life that persists without grand historical hopes, and which has no penchant for Final Things and Days of Judgement.

The deft craftsmanship of *Renfrewshire in Old Photographs* will be appreciated by those who want a poetry which is dedicated to the here-and-now; antiquarians and Brownie Box enthusiasts may, however, be disappointed.

David O' Meara — *Storm Still*
Carleton University Press pbk $12.95
ISBN 0 88629 360 X

THE 'HUMAN EXPERIENCE': don't you just shudder at the mention of it? Angst and unfulfilled promise, those hackneyed tropes of poetic invention, could so easily have infiltrated David O'Meara's *Storm Still* and dragged it into the chattels of existential blathering. Yet his unpretentious style and vivid tableaux of the everyday prevent philosophical reflections from developing beyond a fleeting thought, a flash of insight whilst walking down the road:

grieving for a wholeness you'll never grasp
but only glimpse in fractions
that shimmer
like troutscales in moonlight.

This collection is split into four parts, which, although occasionally darting into historical 're-visions' (such as 'From the diary of Don Antonio' and 'Desert Sonnets'), essentially chart the progression from 'pre-teen terror' to cynical maturity. The breathless anticipation and trepidation of 'Axis Mundi', where naive terror features as a charging bull, grows into transitory enthusiasm in 'Soundings' to culminate finally as the bleak revelation of 'Storm Still'.

With a Heaney-esque ear O'Meara uses language to recreate the relationship between man and the elements. Natural spaces are shown to embody the potential inspiration, the threat of violence, and also become a point of reference, enabling the poet to keep personal experience in perspective. Moving through the collection it is striking how the original fascination develops into a resignation at the inevitable wrench of change and departure. In the penultimate section, 'Desert', the link is at last established between the long running theme of time passing and human mortality:

I know about the time, as a child, you'd
                      stare
Beyond far off cottages on the opposite
                      lakeside
wondering how it would feel to die.
                  Remember?
Do you? You were hardly serious then.

The dark, violent vision of the final section is nevertheless counterbalanced, the echoes of 'Desert Sonnets' and the light-hearted 'Um' and 'Little Boys' prevent me from despairing at the collection's austere terminus.

Marked by an acute self-awareness, *Storm Still* oscillates between the physical and the metaphysical without tangling itself up in either. A profound sense of equilibrium ensures that O'Meara's writing is never terse or turgid, as is beautifully exemplified in the poem 'Turtle Soup'. Darwin's Theory of Evolution, as seen through the eyes of an unenlightened and perplexed sea captain, appears at first to reflect upon the frustration and determina- tion of great minds at work. Joyfully, however, with a Rabelaisan jolt, this 'great mind' is catapulted unequivocally back to the body – the stomach to be precise – as

he chunders his guts out on the poop deck.

Violence is a definite feature of this collection, yet O'Meara has imbued his work with a lyricism that is elegant whilst remaining original and dynamic, despite his insistence that he does not want to 'coast or lilt'. He takes you by the hand and waltzes you through parts of life that have only previously been approached on tiptoe. That is not to say that his writing is irreverent in any way, only that in his contemplation he retains, thankfully, a sense of proportion at all times.

Carol Anderson & Aileen Christianson (eds.) — *Scottish Women's Fiction 1920s to 1960s: Journeys into Being* Tuckwell Press pbk. £9.99 ISBN 1 86232 082 9

THE AMBIGUITIES in the subtitle to this collection are worth dwelling on, since they illuminate both the strengths and weaknesses of many of the essays contained within it. What are we to understand by 'Journeys into Being', itself a reference to Nan Shepherd's *The Living Mountain* ('The journey is itself part of the technique by which the god is sought. It is a journey into Being')?

The most apparent meaning is the most unsatisfactory: that the fiction produced by Scottish women in the period under consideration should be understood in terms of identity — national, regional, but most often, gendered. The editors have pluralised 'journeys', they note, 'to suggest the variety and range of experiences that these women writers explore: the spiritual dimensions as well as the material, the social and historical as well as the metaphysical.' Admirable sentiments, doubtless, but there's a subtle dogmatism at work here.

However 'metaphysical' the novel, it is to be referred to the question of experience, to the factical existence of its author. The marginalisation and isolation of many women writers by the literary establishment in this period is to be repeated by the academic order now, since the primary exegetical factor will be what genitalia the book's author possesses.

Which gives us a clue as to a second interpretation of the subtitle. 'Journeys into Being' is to indicate a prehistory of the intellectual space from which these essays are written; thus the authors become precursors in a refined project of identitarian thought. A typical move, performed in several of the essays, is to acknowledge a difficulty with thinking identity and feminism together, preferably with a brief non-contextualised reference to the canon of feminist thought, before going on to see how the author under consideration has predicted or negotiates this difficulty.

The fact that several of these references are to thinkers who are very much a product of the French post-war reception of Heidegger helps us to what would be a third, and more profitable reading of the subtitle. In this account, 'Journeys into Being' would be precisely the 'spiritual' and 'metaphysical' dimensions of the novels, which the editors have already suggested should be referred back to material experience: that Being *might* (but this must remain an open question) transcend sexual difference is not a possibility that can be considered in this context.

In such a reductive operation, the most complex writers will suffer the most; so I'll take Alison Lumsden's essay on Nan Shepherd as a convenient example. Lumsden reads the spatial metaphors in Shepherd's text as addressing the problem of a woman locating herself in relation to the patriarchal symbolic order, with obligatory reference to Kristeva. For Lumsden Garry Forbes's aunt Barbara Patterson typifies an existence outside the social order; described as 'elemental', 'earthen smelling'. Yet I wonder whether Shepherd doesn't suggest precisely the opposite: Bawbie's earthy qualities are symptomatic of her insertion into the social world at the deepest possible level. Thus when Garry claims that the war hasn't affected Fetter-Rothnie, Bawbie is able to put him right: the country has been affected from the bottom up.

I think it would be possible to argue that what Shepherd offers is an exploration not of the boundaries between the social and the semiotic orders, but drawing on the romantic tradition, of the relationship between man and world which pre-dates the Heideggerian fourfold, distributed along the axes of heaven and earth (Bawbie's earth to Ellen's spiritual realm) and between the (absent) gods and the lives of mortals. This is undoubtedly complicated by gender; and Shepherd is certainly concerned to show the difference in opportunities available to women of different generations. But the final horizon of the work transcends the social order; the challenge of the novel would be to articulate the two together.

Lumsden's essay is typical, if an extreme

case, and I do not wish to play down the pedagogical importance of this book: the authors (and texts) addressed are those who are most regularly taught in Scottish Literature departments — amongst them, Willa Muir, Muriel Spark, Jessie Kesson, Nancy Brysson Morrison, Naomi Mitchison — making this a valuable resource. (And with excellent bibliographical support.) But if this *is* to be a teaching text, the risk that these novelists will become simply an footnote in an account of the coming-to-consciousness of the women's movement may be a high price to pay for their recognition.

Duncan Glen — *Selected Scottish & Other Essays*
Akros pbk £12.95
ISBN 0 86142 101 9

(33 Lady Nairn Avenue, Kirkcaldy, Fife, KY1 2AW)

THERE IS A passage in one of the essays collected here, in which Duncan Glen is writing about Ian Hamilton Finlay, which is highly suggestive about the book as a whole. Glen refers to a letter from Finlay, which has been passed on to one of his students: 'in this letter, which the student did not return to me, we can see that Hamilton Finlay is a brilliant specifier of the final form of a work that he has visualised.' These essays bear witness to the fragility of the cultural artifact, perpetually menaced by the possibility of its own disappearance.

We should read this collection as testimony to that which has occurred; and as messages from an age in which the roles of poet, critic, publisher and academic were not as distinct as they are now. For as editor of *Akros* magazine, as an independent publisher and as a writer, Duncan Glen has worked with and known many of the key figures in Twentieth Century Scottish Literature. So while these essays sometimes walk an uneasy line between anecdote and analysis, between the biographical and the critical, they have a force (and indeed, a clarity) peculiar to their author.

With material on Henderson, Morgan, Goodsir Smith, Soutar, MacDiarmid as well as Frank O'Hara, Tom Scott and Alexander Scott, the volume covers a certain amount of well-trodden ground, as well as being another good resource for the growing academic industry of Scot. Lit. But some of the most interesting material comes in the accounts of the publishing industry in Scotland, and of Scotland's literary magazines. These essays are also the ones which pose (implicitly) the key question; which is that of the future. Since that future is in your hands, and mine — what shall we make of it?

Frances Williams – *Wild Blue*
seren pbk £6.95
ISBN 1 85411 276 7

WILD BLUE IS a substantial collection of poetry from a relatively young poet. Frances Williams's work is haunted by a myth of a Fall – the fall of an apple. In 'Isaac Newton', the great scientist is an Adam who falls when the proverbial apple drops 'Wormless and perfect into/ His aching lap' as he sits in his frustrated 'monkish/ Contemplation', 'his pricks of sweat itching/ At the sinful thoughts he sought to quell.' The real fall, for Williams, is this scientific detachment from bodily being; we are told how Newton's 'mind was alien as a moon/ To his limp limbs.'

Her work therefore tries to escape from the lessons of Newtonian mechanics and optics. In 'Wild Blue', the speaker sits with her lover in the World Trade Centre restaurant, and sees 'Liberty [...]/ Hung like a trinket/ At the edge of your face'. Earlier, though, the scales were reversed:

That day I'd climbed her,
Impatient and panting,
A worm in her chest.

Weight, size, and perspective are concepts barred from the naïve spatiality proper to Williams's psychological Eden. Just as a child will draw a human figure with an enormous head, so her work ascribes magnitude to what is most humanly valuable. The speaker's lover in 'Wild blue' is bigger even than the statue of Liberty – 'Her Colossus shrinks/ as you address me/ In all my diminutive grace' – and, in 'Descent', the immediacy of an inflight meal overpowers an entire landmass:

My cheese cracker is bigger
Than Kangaroo Island. I measure the gap
Between hand and mouth as Melbourne
Fades to Adelaide.

Such devices, however, can prove tiresome. While Williams's verse is certainly metrically accomplished, and linguistically sophisticated, I found her adoption of naïve perceptions, despite their intellectual pedigree, to be more superficial than fresh or provocative.

Tony Lopez — *Data Shadow*
Reality Street Editions pbk £6.50
ISBN 1 874400 17 2

Patricia Farrell, Shelby Matthews, Simon Perril, Keston Sutherland —
New Tonal Language
Reality Street Editions pbk £5.00
ISBN 1 874400 18 0

(Reality Street Editions, 4 Howard Court, Peckham Rye, London SE15 3PH)

The advent of multi-channel TV has provided a wonderful means for describing some of the more fragmentary and plurivocal forms of contemporary poetry; those in which diffuse and dissonant voices intermingle or cut across each other. All we have to do is think of such poetry as a late-night channel surfing spree, perhaps slightly intoxicated. But I wonder whether the ease with which we can deploy this imagery doesn't in turn suggest the limits of the kind of poetry which evokes it.

Indeed, this may be the case with Tony Lopez, whose *Data Shadow* collection seems to be concerned with precisely this contradiction; that the fragmentation of contemporary experience demands a poetic form which can render it unfamiliar, but without surrendering itself to mere affirmation of the economic and social values dissolved in the flux of information. The formal device of the sonnet struggles here to contain the dischordant vocal ranges, such as this juxtaposition: 'Nothing works like repression in fixed circuits / To carry signals to the heart. Enjoys music,/

Gardening, cinema, seeks funny male/
Who must be genuine.'

Prefaced with a polemical intro which
suggests 'Let's improvise a negation of
negation in four-four time' it's hard not to
come to the conclusion of the poem with a
sense of exhaustion at the restless energy of
the sequence: 'Tick if you would / prefer
not to receive any more of this material.'

New Tonal Language is the fourth of
Reality Street's four-packs, but all the poets
share Lopez's concern with wrestling the
language of poetry into new configurations.
I particularly enjoyed Shelby Matthews
loose ambles across the page; but all the
poets included deserve close attention.

**David Kinloch & Richard Price (eds.)
— *La Nouvelle Alliance: Influences
francophones sur la littérature ecossaise
moderne*
ELLUG pbk 140 F
ISBN 2 84310 021 6**

**(ELLUG, Université Stendhal, BP 25,
38040 GRENOBLE CEDEX 9)**

**Henry Mackenzie — *Julia de Roubigné*
Tuckwell pbk. £9.99
ISBN 1 86232 047 0**

IT WAS ONLY really a matter of time before
someone got around to proclaiming a
renewal of the Auld Alliance; but I'm glad
that it's been done with such authority and
flair by David Kinloch and Richard Price.
The contributors to their collection of
essays address the topic from a range of
different angles, but without any kind of
dogmatism.

Most of the essays focus on questions of

individual influence: for example Alan
Riach writes on MacDiarmid and Valéry;
Robin Purves connects Isidore Ducasse to
Frank Kuppner via Lautreamont. Two
interesting essays take up writers from
relatively marginalised French language
communities. Christopher Whyte looks at
what Sidney Goodsir-Smith found in the
Breton poet Tristan Corbière, while David
Kinloch looks at Scots translations of
Michel Tremblay.

The editors have chosen a non-
programmatic approach, and in their
introduction admit the provisional nature
of their selection — Kenneth White
makes an appearance, but no Alex Trocchi
— which suggests this is a beginning for a
continuing process of translation. Indeed,
Paul Barnaby's revealing essay explores
precisely which writers have been translated into French, and concludes posi-
tively, with increasing interest in Scottish
writers in France. Barnaby's approach is an
interesting complement to the more
literary essays, based as it is on the
empirical work of the BOSLIT project at
the National Library — but given the
book's title, a similarly empirical look at
what came the other way, if you like,
would be even more useful.

Tuckwell's reprint of Henry Mackenzie's
third novel, *Julia de Roubigné* also joins
Scottish and French writing. As Susan
Manning points out in her excellent
introduction, like the better-known *Man
of Feeling*, this is an ambiguous but
intriguing response to the sensational
psychologism of some eighteenth-century
French works. (The title is presumed to
allude to Rousseau.) Does setting the
novel in France imply that this the novel is

supposed to be a bad example as such, or that English-speaking readers will only believe the melodramatic self-absorption and fatal, all-consuming passions of the characters if they're French?

It's more consistent and less intellectualised than *The Man of Feeling* but more psychologically intense; and thus adds yet another side to our understanding of Scottish Literature of the eighteenth century.

292: Essays in Visual Culture
free (£2 p&p), twice yearly

(*292*, Faculty of Art & Design, Edinburgh College of Art, Lauriston Place, Edinburgh, EH3 9DF)

Metronome No. 4-5-6
price on request, appears irregularly

(Contact: proto academy (Edinburgh Projects), Edinburgh College of Art, Lauriston Place, EH3 9DF)

I DON'T KNOW whether it's just envy warping my perceptions, but there seems to be a staggering amount of subsidy sloshing around for the visual arts: and the green-eyed monster really comes to stay when the visual and the textual meet. I suspect that's why these two journal issues have impressed themselves upon me so much.

292 bills itself as a new arrival on the art publishing scene in Scotland, and is subtitled 'Essays in Visual Culture'. Given away free (two pounds postage and packaging an issue) it shouldn't have any trouble building up its circulation. Despite the fact that each issue has an avowed theme, it appears thoroughly miscellaneous, but I often have trouble wondering which is the text and which the artist's pages.

It's printed on thick paper and lovely to handle and must be subsidised to all hell. Clearly a write-off from the research section of Edinburgh College of Art it swamps its attempt to re-establish an essay tradition with some gorgeous artists pages, with work from Ian Hamilton Finlay and Chad McCail amongst others. The essays struggle to catch up, especially since they're laid out in a rather drab Helvetica-looking typeface.

Metronome is similarly hefty, but its bulk is its thickness rather than its page size. In fact it is modelled on an old edition of Francis Jeffrey's *Edinburgh Review*, with a gratifying nod to this version of the periodical in the back, although few of the contributions seem to acknowledge this. It's basically a hand-held, portable, ensemble exhibition, drawing on artists from across Europe.

As you might expect, some of it is fascinating and thought-provoking; some of it is tedious, incomprehensible, or clearly knocked up by some art student from the photographs that they had left on the floor of the studio. That however, must be the risk taken to produce something new, and I can confidently say that I have never seen anything like this before in my life.

If you're interested in getting hold of it, the bookshop at the Fruitmarket Gallery might be able to help you, as they have had copies in stock.

REVIEWS BY Joe Marshall, Katy Mahood, Gavin Miller, Daniel Mittler, Matthew Reason and Alex Thomson

Back issues available

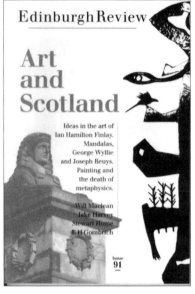

Issue 91: Art and Scotland,

including:
Ideas in the Art of Ian Hamilton Finlay; Murdo Macdonald on the social space in Scottish Art; Alan Woods on E.H. Gombrich; Duncan Macmillan on Painting and the Death of Metaphysics; articles on Will Maclean, Jake Harvey, George Wyllie and Joseph Beuys

Other issues available include:

Issue 101: *Exchanges,*
  featuring work by David Bellingham

Issue 98: *more boreal*
  including Ian Stephen's Vital Memorials; Ian McKeever

Issue 94: *Cosmorama* (last few copies)
  featuring George Wylie; Artist's books in Scotland

All back issues cost £5, inc. postage and packaging, available from Edinburgh Review, 22a Buccleuch Place, Edinburgh, EH8 9LF. Full list of back issues also available on request.

Subscribe to *Edinburgh Review*

SUBSCRIBING TO EDINBURGH REVIEW
• Guarantees delivery of the best new writing in Scotland, direct to your door.
• Brings you the best new critical thought in Britain.
• Keeps you informed about the latest work from the small press world.
• Ensures you receive all three issues a year.
• Is still cheaper than buying the magazine in a bookshop.
• Costs onl;y £17 a year for individuals, £34 for institutions

BACK ISSUES are also available at a discount rate, please contact our office for more information or to place an order

SUBSCRIPTION FORM

Name:
Address:

Postcode:

I wish to subscribe to the Edinburgh Review, beginning from issue 105 / ___ .
* I enclose a cheque made for £17 (individual) / £34 (institutional) made payable to 'Edinburgh Review'
* I wish to pay by Credit / Debit Card, details below:
[* = delete as applicable]

Type of Card: VISA / Mastercard / Switch [Delete as appropriate]

Card Number:

Card Valid from: _ / _ / _ To: _ / _ / _ Issue No: _ [Switch Only]

Signature:_____   Date: _ / _ / _

Please complete and return form to Edinburgh Review, 22a Buccleuch Place, Edinburgh, EH8 9LN